Stuffed Tomatoes (recipe page 33)

How do you like them apples?

Foreword

Healthy eating should be fun and enjoyable - as well as a way of life.

This is the philosophy of Ian Parmenter,presenter of the ABC television series "Consuming Passions" and author of this book.

Ian has indulged his consuming passion for food by putting together more than 100 of his favourite recipes.

This book will dispel any lingering doubts that healthy food can be both appetising and delicious.

From the ABC Televison series.

Published by Consuming Passions Pty Ltd
in association with the
ABC Enterprises for the
AUSTRALIAN BROADCASTING CORPORATION
700 Harris Street, Ultimo NSW 2007

Text, illustrations and photography:
© Copyright Consuming Passions Pty Ltd 1992

Consuming Passions
ISBN 1 875545 06 9

Written and illustrated by Ian Parmenter

Design and photography by Paul Johnson

All photographs taken with Nikon cameras and
lenses on Kodak Ektachrome film

Coordination by Sue Robertson

Kind assistance from Dale Ednie-Brown,
Anne Hay and Kate Moore

Research by Ann Dewar and Jackie O'Connell

Printed in Singapore by Toppan

Consuming Passions gratefully
acknowledges the generous support and
commitment provided by the following:

Australian Airlines

Australian Broadcasting Corporation

Australian Chicken Meat Federation

Australian Horticulture Corporation

Australian Pork Corporation

Canned Food Information Service Inc

Gascoyne Produce Marketing Association

International Olive Oil Council

K.F.M Fisheries Pty Ltd

Kodak Australasia

Maxwell Optical Industries (Nikon)

Miele Australia

National Heart Foundation of Australia

North Tasmania Aquaculture Pty Ltd

Oriel Brasserie

Peter Lehmann Wines

Primary Product Promotions of W. A.

Ricegrowers Co-operative Ltd

Select Hotels

Tasmanian Development Authority

Telecom Australia

The Queen Victoria Market

Western Australian Ministry for Agriculture

Western Australian Ministry for Fisheries

About the Author

Ian Parmenter was born in post-war London and survived nine years of British cooking before his parents moved to Belgium and, to his great relief, took him with them.

In Brussels, the city famous for its sprouts, he began his love affair with food. The Belgian national dish of chips with mayonnaise was the first he learnt to master.

His adventures with continental cuisine were curtailed when he was sent back to England to further his education at an ancient British school, where he was forced to eat ancient British food, such as hot tinned pilchards on toast. He had to develop his cooking skills secretly in the chemistry lab with a bunsen burner, fish fingers and baked beans. He claims his fish finger and baked bean casserole cooked in a conical flask is still remembered with great affection by the year of '64.

On graduation, Ian began a career in journalism which took him to Fleet Street's better eating and drinking establishments, where he remained for 7 years - long enough to acquire the itch.

His palate jaded by years of smoked mackerel paté and ploughman's lunches, Ian fled to Australia arriving in the early seventies, a period not known for its sophisticated food culture. He remembers one of his first hotel breakfasts being lamb chops, fried eggs, bacon, beetroot and cold lumpy gravy washed down with weak black instant coffee with a slice of orange rind in it.

Joining the ABC in 1973, Ian soon moved into television production and has since been responsible for producing such programmes as Rock Arena, Talking Pictures, the 1986

ABC Sports Awards, the 1987 America's Cup coverage and the 1990 AFI Awards. He has also produced four Leeuwin Estate concerts, two of which won Penguin Awards.

Consuming Passions is his first venture in front of the camera, a position he says is like being an animal liberationist at a duck shooters' dinner.

With the first series now completed, Ian has begun work on a new season's shows, which will continue his quest to get Australians and Australian produce into Australian kitchens and to demonstrate that cooking can always be fun - or else!

Many of this book's recipes are from the television series.

His previous writings include "Fish Smoking - the Passive Way", "1001 Meals Without Mince" and "Microwaving Your Friends Goodbye". Surprisingly, these works are yet to be published.

He lists his hobbies as playing guitar, harmonica and piano - but not necessarily in that order - and spending all his money on food and wine.

He lives in Fremantle with his wife, Ann, and three extremely well-fed cats.

Contents

Introduction

Most of us are passionate about good food and when it comes to good food Australia is certainly the place to be. With our climate and soil types we are able to produce the widest possible range of foods and beverages. Our meats, fish and seafoods, fruit and vegetables, cereals, herbs and spices, wine and beer, even tea and coffee are of a quality to rival the world's best.

For the last two hundred years migrants have been bringing with them their foods and traditions, sharing their secrets so that Australians may now enjoy some of the finest dishes from around the world. And at last the foods of the bush are making an appearance in shops, markets and restaurants so that we are discovering such taste sensations as lemon aspen, bush tomatoes, wild rosella, and lilli pilli.

The "Consuming Passions" television series and this book aim to show that being able to prepare food well is something we can all do. There are no secrets. Beautiful meals are within reach of all of us. And above all I hope to show that cooking needn't be a chore. It should always be fun.

In this book there's a wide range of recipes from the traditional to the new, from simple breads to a delightful dish of fish with pawpaw sauce.

The recipes are all simple. Many traditional recipes have been modified to suit the busy, health-conscious society of the nineties, and new ones keep in mind the need to watch our intake of saturated fats and salt. Invaluable advice on nutrition has been provided by the National Heart Foundation.

I hope that with "Consuming Passions" you will to share my passion for good food.

Off the shelf...

It happens to all of us at some time or other - after aerobics, golf or the theatre you hear a voice say "Why not come back to my place for a bite to eat?" You realise with horror that it was your voice and suddenly you're faced with the prospect of feeding half-a-dozen people. I'm always catering for groups of people at short notice and it's in these situations I need easy-to-prepare recipes using the ingredients I have in the pantry or fridge. Many of this book's recipes are designed for just that sort of situation. The following are what I recommend you have at home as part of the kitchen arsenal:

Pastas. I like to keep a range which includes some egg noodles as well as traditional spaghetti, macaroni and lasagne sheets.

Olive oil. I use it almost exclusively as it is low in saturated fat. I keep extra virgin oil for dishes which benefit from the olive flavour. For frying I use extra light oil, which has hardly any discernible flavour. You can also use canola (rape seed oil), another predominantly unsaturated oil, but remember, whichever oil you use, it is still a fat and should be used sparingly.

Sesame oil. A few droplets added to a rice or vegetable dish can make all the difference to the flavour of the dish.

Olives. Useful as appetisers as well as in cooking, olives are available in tins and jars. Once opened, they keep for several days in the refrigerator.

Tinned tomatoes. Always useful in soups and sauces.

Garlic and onions. Both keep very well. When buying them make sure they feel firm. Look for large cloves in the garlic.

Ginger. Root ginger is now readily available. It keeps very well. Just break off a small piece, skin and slice thinly or grate.

Soy sauce. One of the oldest sauces, it's now one of the world's most popular. I prefer the reduced salt variety.

Stock. There is nothing like making your own stock, which keeps very well in the deep freeze. I also keep a few tins of broth or consommé on hand.

Lemons. Both the juice and the grated rind of the lemon are terrific flavour boosters.

Herbs. Two words of advice - grow them. There are many essential herbs that most of us could grow: bay, thyme, oregano, rosemary, parsley, sage, basil and coriander. I rarely use dried herbs, which can easily overpower dishes.

Spices. Unless you're going to specialise in Indian and Asian cuisine, don't rush out to buy the complete range. The ones I most commonly use are nutmeg (whole), five spice, cloves, mixed spice, cumin and chilli.

Nuts. Useful additions to many vegetable, fruit and rice dishes, I keep hazelnuts, almonds and pine nuts, but buy pistachios, pecans and walnuts when I need them.

Sweeteners. Honey, raw sugar, and soft brown sugar.

Anchovies. A tin or jar is indispensable for a special salad, soup, pizza or pasta dish. Look for Australian anchovies which have a lower salt content.

Pulses. It's a good idea to keep a supply of dried beans and lentils. They keep well.

Parmesan. A hard cooked curd cheese aged for 2 to 3 years, it keeps very well in block form and because of its strong flavour only a small amount is needed. Best grated immediately before use.

You are bound to have some fresh vegetables in the kitchen which, combined with some of the above, will give you all you need to make many of this book's recipes.

Breads

Consult a dozen cookery books and you will find a dozen different recipes for bread. There is no perfect recipe for bread, any more than there is a perfect recipe for anything else. The variations are limitless.

What is generally agreed is that bread is a mixture of flour, water, salt and yeast which is allowed to prove and then is baked. And at its simplest that is what bread is.

There are no great mysteries and no real difficulties in making beautiful bread in your own kitchen.

Bread is also rewarding to make and can be therapeutic. Kneading dough is a great way of relieving tension.

My basic bread recipe uses those usual elements, flour, water, salt and yeast, plus I add oil to give a softer, spongier texture and some sugar to give flavour and help the yeast do its work. As well as great variation in the quantities of ingredients used in bread making, there are also many different techniques which can be applied.

These are a few simple guidelines to making, baking and storing your own bread:

Flour. Any flour may be used but plain is preferred for a lighter loaf. Most plain flours are 'all purpose', a mixture of hard wheat flour, which is perfect for bread and pasta making, and soft wheat flour better for pastries and puddings. So it is a compromise. If you can get bread flour, so much the better.

Salt. Salt adds flavour but it retards the proving process. For the best results when making your bread, don't overdo it.

Yeast. Many cooks worry about using it, yet it is user-friendly and performs well if treated properly. Yeast is a living organism which causes dough to rise by converting flour's natural sugars into carbon dioxide bubbles trapped in the dough. These bubbles expand during baking to give the bread its texture. Either dried or fresh yeast may be used. The ideal temperature for its use is 30°C. Yeast will die at or above 54°C.

Water. Like yeast, 30°C is the ideal temperature for the water you use in the bread mix. If you are uncertain about the temperature, test it by putting in a finger. If it feels just cool to touch it will be suitable. It is better to err on the side of cooler water.

Oil. I like to use olive oil in my bread dough. A light, subtle flavoured oil for sweet bread, a strongly flavoured virgin oil for savoury breads, especially pizzas.

Sugar. As well as its flavouring quality, the addition of sugar will assist the yeast's action.

Proving. The proving process is where the light texture of bread is formed. Bread dough made with plain flour should prove for between 3/4 hour and 1 hour depending on the room temperature. The warmer the room, the less time will be needed for proving. It should double in size during proving and this is best done in a warm place with the dough in a bowl covered with a damp tea towel. A dough proved twice will make a better loaf.

Kneading. This is an important operation which induces elasticity into the dough and promotes a smooth even texture. Usually kneading need not take more than five minutes. It should be done on a floured surface, with enthusiasm. When kneaded, the dough should be elastic.

Baking tins. There must be plenty of hot air circulation around the bread and its tin during baking. Bread, cake and brioche tins, scone trays, pizza pans, even flower pots (as long as they are well cleaned and oiled) are suitable. I always lubricate the containers with a light smear of olive oil.

Topping. Once in the containers the bread shapes may be topped to give colour and texture. Without any topping the bread will be matt brown. A light dusting of flour will give a more attractive mix of brown and white. Egg yolk will give a yellow gloss while egg white will give a lighter gloss. It's a good idea to experiment with egg, water, milk, flour and sugar-water toppings and adopt the ones you prefer.

Baking. A baking temperature of 220°C is ideal. The oven should not be opened until the bread has started browning. By this time the yeast will have ceased its operation.

Testing. The best test for *doneness* is to tap the bottom of the loaf. If it sounds hollow it will be cooked. If not, put it back into the tin and back into the oven for a few more minutes.

Cooling. When cooked the bread should be taken out of the tin and put on a wire rack to cool. It will have a crisp crust. If you prefer a softer crust cover the bread with a cloth as it cools.

Storing. The higher the fat and sugar content of a bread, the longer it will stay fresh. Usually, fresh home baked bread is best eaten the day it is baked, which it usually is!

It may also be frozen for several days. Cut it into thick slices before wrapping and freezing.

SIMPLE WHITE BREAD

Makes 1 loaf or 12 rolls

1 kg plain white flour
50 g fresh yeast or
2 packets dry yeast (14 or 15 g)
1 tbsp sugar
2 tspn salt
750 mls water
1 tbsp oil

Dissolve sugar, yeast and 2 tbsp flour in a little water and mix well.

Put remainder of flour in a large bowl. Stir in yeast mixture. Add water to make up a stiff dough. Mix well and stir in the oil. Cover bowl with damp tea towel and leave to prove in a warm place until it has doubled in size (between 45 minutes and an hour).

Remove the mixture from the bowl and knead well on floured surface for about 5 minutes.

Shape into loaf or rolls, put into oiled bread tins or onto a baking tray.

Cover again with cloth and allow to prove

for a further 45 minutes.

Sprinkle with flour. Bake in oven at 220°C for about 45 minutes (large loaves) or 20 minutes (rolls)

Test by tapping bottoms. If they sound hollow, they're cooked!

One of the best ways of enjoying freshly baked bread is by eating it warm, dipped into virgin olive oil mixed with crushed garlic and freshly ground black pepper.

CALZONE
The Italian Pastie

A pizza with a difference.

The difference is that instead of putting a topping on a bread base, as you do with a conventional pizza, with a calzone the topping becomes the filling and goes inside to make something close to our own familiar pastie.

The key elements in our filling are ham and cheese - both available with a reduced fat content.

The wrapping is simply a bread dough.

Makes 2 calzone and serves 6 as a main meal

500 g bread dough which has been proved for an hour

1 small low fat mozzarella cheese (or packet of grated mozzarella)

350 g lean ham

1/2 tspn grated nutmeg

1 tbsp fresh oregano (or 1/2 tspn dried oregano)

Olive oil to lubricate pan

To prepare the filling, chop the ham into small cubes, or if it is bought sliced, cut into strips. Chop the mozzarella into similar small cubes, unless you are using grated packet mozzarella, which will do just as well.

Put both into mixing bowl with nutmeg and finely chopped oregano and toss together.

To assemble calzone, smear a little olive oil over baking tray (such as a pizza tray), knead dough and cut into halves. Roll out one piece of dough until it is big enough to cover a dinner plate.

Put on oiled baking tray and add half the ham and cheese mix to one side leaving some space where the dough will seal.

Fold other side of dough over the mixture and press the dough together to make a bond. Rub a little plain flour over the top to add a little character. And that's it! Ready for the oven.

You may also put some fresh herbs on the tray when it goes into the oven. The flavours will gently travel into the calzone during baking.

Repeat the process with the other piece of dough and remaining mixture.

Bake in a hot oven at about 225°C for about 30 minutes. The calzone will tell you when they are ready by sending fantastic aromas wafting through the kitchen.

Serve with a huge salad.

Herbal hint: Oregano and sage should be treated with respect. They have bold flavours and should be used sparingly.

BRUSCHETTA WITH TOMATOES

The Tuscans of Italy would be offended if we didn't inform you of their name for this dish. We call it bruschetta, as the folk of Umbria do, but the Tuscans call it fettunta. There is no real difference between the two, both are thick slices of crusty bread, anointed with oil, and topped with tomatoes. Delicious!

Serves 6 to 9

18 pieces of crusty bread, cut into slices, 2-3 cm thick

2 cloves of garlic, peeled and halved
Handful of basil leaves
1/2 cup extra virgin olive oil
Freshly ground, black pepper
2 large ripe, but not over-ripe, tomatoes

Preheat oven to 200°C.

Put the slices of bread on the shiny side of a piece of flat, aluminium foil. Toast them in the oven for 10 minutes on each side.

Then rub both sides of the bread with garlic.

Arrange the basil leaves on a large platter, put the pieces of bread over them.

Warm the oil over a very low heat.

Then brush it over the bread. Season with pepper to taste. Slice the tomatoes horizontally. Cut each slice in half. Place each half-slice on top of each slice of bread. Sprinkle with freshly ground black pepper. Serve immediately.

BRUSCHETTA WITH MUSHROOMS

Serves 6

18 pieces of bread
(as in previous recipe)
100 g fresh mushrooms, thinly sliced
1 cup water
1 tbsp olive oil
4 garlic cloves, crushed
4 tbsp white wine
1/2 tbsp fresh thyme, chopped
1/2 tbsp fresh rosemary, chopped
Freshly ground black pepper
4 tbsp fresh parsley, chopped
4 tbsp fresh lemon juice

Heat the olive oil in a large skillet, add garlic and gently sauté for 2 to 4 minutes. Add mushrooms.

Sauté, stirring for another minute or two, then add white wine.

Continue cooking until the wine has just about evaporated, then add water, thyme, rosemary, and freshly ground pepper.

Increase the heat to high and continue cooking until almost all of the liquid has evaporated, stirring constantly.

Stir in 3 tbsp of parsley and the lemon juice.

Top the bread with this mixture, sprinkle with the remaining parsley, and serve immediately.

FRENCH STYLE PIZZA

Surprising though it may seem, there is a belief that the pizza was invented by the French.

True, in the south of France there is an ancient form of pizza called Pissaladiere.

However, it is more likely that it was introduced by the Roman cooks in Avignon before the French could think of it.

This recipe for a French pizza is perfect for those who know - and like - their onions.

Serves 4 to 6

500 g bread dough
(see page 11)
3 tbsp good olive oil
6 cups sliced onions
4 to 5 garlic cloves, peeled, crushed and chopped
100 g anchovy fillets
A handful of black olives

Preheat the oven to 200°C.

Heat the oil in a saucepan and add the onions. Cook on low heat for about 20 minutes, until the onions are well cooked. Add the garlic, then the pepper.

Now spread the dough out by hand so it is the size of a 40 cm by 30 cm baking tray.

Oil the baking tray. Now spread the dough out with your hands so that it lines the tray. The dough should be a little less than a centimetre thick.

Spread the cooked onions on the dough. Place the anchovies in a criss-cross pattern on top.

Remove the pips from the olives, cut them in half, then position one in each anchovy diamond.

Sprinkle the 'pizza' with 1 tbsp of olive oil and bake for 30 minutes.

FOCACCIA WITH SWEET RED CAPSICUM

Some people deny themselves the pleasure of eating this wonderful Genoese pizza because of the unfounded notion that it is going to be a fattening experience.

To destroy the myth, and let those of you who are sworn off focaccia eat it, I have researched its nutritional content.

Focaccia has about the same kilojoules as bread, depending on what you add to it when cooked.

Makes 1 large focaccia for 6

1 red capsicum

3 cups white flour

1 tbsp dried yeast

2 cups tepid water

*1 tspn fresh thyme, chopped or 1/2 tspn
dried thyme*

1 tbsp olive oil

Roast the capsicum in the oven and remove skin. (See Capsicum Caper on page 42) Chop it into small dice and set aside.

Dissolve the yeast in water. Gradually add flour until it pulls away from the sides, add capsicum, and then thyme. Knead lightly.

Oil a flat pan 2 cm deep, 35 cm across.

With oiled hands pat down dough into pan, dimpling top with fingertips. Cover with a damp cloth and allow to sit until doubled.

Sprinkle with a little extra thyme then bake in a hot oven (220°C) until golden.

Focaccia can be substituted for bread and made into a sandwich, or eaten with pasta, meat dishes or salad.

SCHIACCIATA

Sweet pizzas are as much fun to make as the savoury variety.

In Italy a favourite is schiacciata, a fruit pizza made with grapes, traditionally during vintage. It is one of the simplest combinations, bread dough and grapes combined to make a tasty and inexpensive dessert.

Serves 6 to 8

*500 gms of bread dough proved for an
hour (see page 11)*

*500 gms grapes (I use red and white
grapes for visual impact)*

1/2 cup raw or brown sugar

Wash grapes, drain and toss with half the sugar.

I use them whole, seeds included because I don't mind the crunchiness but if it worries you, you can either use the seedless variety or find someone to seed them for you.

Prepare a pizza pan or similar flat tray. Just smear with a little light oil.

Simple White Bread (recipe page 11)

Bruschetta with Tomatoes and Mushrooms (recipe pages 13 and 14)

Focaccia with Sweet Red Capsicum (recipe page 15)

Schiacciata (recipe page 16)

Now divide the dough into two and roll out the first of two base shapes for what will become a grape sandwich.

You don't have to worry about making a perfect circle - rough enough is good enough. Put it onto the oiled pan.

Dot some of the grapes over the base leaving some space between them. Sprinkle on a little more sugar.

Roll a second base shape.

Place it over the first layer pushing down around the edge to seal it.

Add more of the grapes, pushing them in the valleys formed by the grapes underneath, and sprinkle with remainder of the sugar.

Bake in a hot oven at 220°C for about 40 minutes.

While it's cooking you might care to make a very tasty accompaniment for the schiacciata.

I make one called Ricotta Delight and you will find it on page 136.

TURKISH CORN BREAD

A yeastless bread using polenta (corn meal) as a base, and natural yoghurt which gives it a slightly sour-dough flavour.

Makes 2 loaves

250 gms polenta (cornmeal)
125 gms plain wholemeal flour
2 tspn baking powder
2 tspn sugar
350 gms low-fat natural yoghurt
2 large eggs
2 tbsp olive oil

Thoroughly mix polenta, wholemeal flour, sugar and baking powder.

Beat eggs, add olive oil and yoghurt. Mix well. Stir in the other ingredients.

Put mixture into 2 lightly oiled bread tins or a high sided cake tin and bake for about 30 minutes at 200°C.

Test for *doneness* by inserting a skewer or satay stick. It should come out cleanly.

Allow to cool for a few minutes before transferring the bread to a wire rack.

Allow to cool almost completely before cutting and serving with strongly flavoured soups or casseroles.

NAAN BREAD

My favourite Indian leavened bread which may be made without yeast with this simplified recipe from Singapore, centre of some of the world's finest Indian food.

It is a perfect accompaniment to Indian curries.

Makes 6

300 g plain flour (preferably strong bread flour)
100 mls low-fat natural yoghurt
2 tbsp light olive oil
Sprinkle of salt
1 beaten egg
1 tspn baking powder

Sift flour into mixing bowl. Add baking powder, salt and stir in beaten egg, yoghurt and 1 tbsp oil.

Mix well. Turn onto clean, floured work surface and knead.

If the mixture is too sloppy, add more flour.

If it is too crumbly, add a little water.

Knead for at least 5 minutes.

Cover with a damp tea towel and leave in a warm, draught-free place for between 2 and 3 hours.

Knead again for a couple of minutes adding more flour if it sticks.

Divide into half a dozen pieces and roll each piece into a 25 cm long oval.

Heat a heavy frying pan smeared with oil.

Cook the naan one by one:

Put piece in pan, dab down on bread with clean damp tea towel.

After a couple of minutes the underside should be browning and the bread should have puffed up a little.

Turn over and repeat process.

When cooked put in warm oven. Serve warm.

Pasta

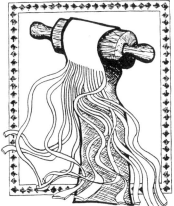

If I were stranded on a desert island and only allowed a certain number of foods, pasta would be right up there at the top of my list, along with the wonderful ingredients which work so well with it: tomatoes, olive oil, garlic, anchovies and basil.

The word pasta comes from the Italian for paste and that's what it is, a paste of flour and either water or eggs.

We always associate pasta with Italy, and although its origins are not known, most food historians believe it was probably created in different places at different times by different cultures.

There's evidence of its existence as long ago as 400 BC and for the past several centuries pasta has been widely used in Asia as well as Europe. Curiously, despite its long history in Europe, its popularity in Anglo-Saxon cuisine has only happened this century.

In England during my childhood the only two available pastas were spaghetti and macaroni, usually treated as nursery food and always served on toast.

The best pasta is made with durum semolina, which is now produced in Australia but not yet widely available to the general public, though it's time we applied some pressure. Wheat flour is also used.

Pasta is wrongly regarded as fattening food, because of its high carbohydrate content. However, it is what accompanies pasta that is usually more fattening.

In the following recipes you will find sauces that are all low in fat content.

HOME MADE PASTA

If you can get it, the best flour for this job is durum semolina, from which most Italian pastas are made.

It's a stronger flour than everyday household plain flour, although that will do. It's best if the flour is unbleached.

Serves 4 to 6

300 g flour

3 large eggs

Grated nutmeg (optional)

Chopped parsley or cooked spinach (optional)

Additional flour for dusting work surface

On a work surface make a small hill of flour. Make a well in the centre. Break in the eggs.

Stir them up with a fork or with your fingers. Its a good idea to have a spatula standing by because the eggs usually want to take off through the wall of your crater and you'll have to round them up.

Gradually add a little flour to the eggs from the inside of the crater.

When the mixture stops being runny you can tumble the rest of the flour over the egg and flour mix.

Then knead lightly with your finger tips until you have a firm dough.

If the eggs are very large you may find the mixture is a bit sloppy. You can add a bit more flour but not too much or your dough will be crumbly.

Make the dough into a ball and put aside while you clean up the work surface and your hands.

Now it's time to knead the dough for 5 or 6 minutes.

If you want, you can add herbs or spice at this stage. I like to add a little cooked spinach or chopped parsley for colour and grated nutmeg.

All sorts of ingredients are added to give colour and flavour: tomato pureé, even chocolate. Yes, it's true.

Now make dough into a bun shape.

Dust the work surface with flour and this is where the fun part begins: The rolling.

For this job I prefer to use a wooden rolling pin.

Roll the dough starting from about a third of the way in and rolling away from you.

Turn it a quarter turn after every roll.

Try to keep it as round as possible.

For making a simple ribbon pasta, such as fettucine or tagliatelle, the pasta should be allowed to dry slightly.

A good way of doing this is to hang it over the rolling pin resting between two chairs.

It should hang long enough to get leathery. About 30 minutes on a cold day or about 3 minutes on a hot Australian summer's day!

Then you roll up pasta like a newspaper. If it is a bit sticky dust it lightly with flour. It should be feeling leathery.

When it's rolled up, simply cut through the roll to the thickness that you would like.

Then gently pull the strands apart and let them dry for a few minutes before cooking.

Do not disturb them too much at this stage or they will break.

Gather them up and toss into lots of boiling water. Stir occasionally with a wooden spoon.

A word of caution. It only takes seconds to cook fresh pasta.

Make sure it doesn't overcook. Try the bite test - it should be firm but not doughy.

Drain and serve with a sauce of your choice.

I prefer a light tomato sauce with a sprinkling of parsley, parmesan and freshly ground black pepper.

PASTA WITH ANCHOVY SAUCE

Here's an easy recipe which can be prepared virtually anywhere.

I once cooked it for the crew of a fishing boat in the Indian Ocean off the coast of Western Australia near Fremantle, where anchovies were being caught.

Serves 4

1 medium onion

2 or 3 cloves of garlic

1 red capsicum

2 tbsp black olives (pitted)

2 tbsp chopped anchovies

A few small chillies or 1 tspn chilli sauce

100 g parmesan cheese

1 tbsp olive oil (preferably extra virgin)

200 g spaghetti (cooked and tossed in a little olive oil)

1/2 tspn grated nutmeg

Chop the onion and capsicum roughly, and crush the peeled garlic cloves. Gently cook in the olive oil over low heat. They won't need much cooking - it's better if the garlic and the onion are still a little crunchy.

Chop the black olives and add to the pan.

Add the anchovies, the chillies or the chilli sauce, and stir in half the grated parmesan cheese.

Toss the cooked spaghetti with the other ingredients in the pan.

Once well mixed with the spaghetti, add pepper to taste and some freshly grated nutmeg (always a great addition to pasta). Don't use salt! There will be enough in the anchovies.

Top with a sprinkling of parmesan cheese and serve with a lightly dressed green salad.

EXPLODING A MYTH

There is a widely held belief that you can test whether pasta is cooked by throwing a piece of it at the wall. If it sticks to the wall it is cooked...or so the story goes.

*Well, apart from the fact that throwing food at walls is best left to babies, it's not a reliable method for testing pasta (or anything else, including roast joints of meat). The best test is to try a piece. It should still have bite to it - as the Italians say, **al dente**.*

PENNE VODKA

One of the most useful assets for any cook is an easy but effective recipe for a meal which can be prepared almost anywhere with ingredients which do not have to be fresh or refrigerated.

This is a simple combination of tubular pasta, penne, and a tomato sauce which is guaranteed to delight just about anyone. It was inspired by Italian expatriate Ernesto Sirolli.

All the ingredients are the sort of things that may be kept in the pantry for those emergencies where you are suddenly called upon to perform a minor miracle.

Serves 6

1 packet penne

2 tins tomatoes

1 large onion finely chopped

A few cloves garlic finely chopped

(or dried garlic flakes)

1/2 tspn grated nutmeg

2 tspn sugar

2 dried chillies or 1 tspn chilli sauce

1/2 tspn black pepper

2 tbsp vodka

2 tbsp olive oil

Parmesan cheese

Boil pasta in lots of water for 12 minutes or according to instructions on packet.

It should still be *al dente*.

Drain and toss in 1 tbsp oil. Set aside. Put remaining oil in pan over medium heat. Cook onion until it becomes clear then add the garlic. Add tinned tomatoes, lower heat to a simmer and reduce the sauce to about a third of its original volume.

Stir in sugar, chilli to taste, grated nutmeg, vodka and black pepper. Cook for 2 minutes to boil off the alcohol. Mix thoroughly and stir in the penne. Serve sprinkled with parmesan cheese.

SHELL PASTA AND BROCCOLI

This is a delicious winter dish. But beware - it has one whole chilli in it. If you forget to take it out before serving, someone will end up with a mighty hot tongue.

Serves 4

500 g blanched broccoli

1 packet shell pasta

1 garlic clove, crushed

1 red chilli

2 tbsp olive oil

Freshly ground black pepper

A little mozzarella cheese

De-seed the chilli, then skewer it firmly with two cocktail sticks inserted diagonally.

This will enable you to find it more easily when you have cooked it.

Heat the oil in a large pan, add the garlic and chilli and cook until the garlic has coloured to a pale gold.

Turn up the heat then add the cooked broccoli.

Fry for 2 or 3 minutes then reduce the heat and cook gently for 5 minutes.

Cook the pasta while the broccoli is cooking, then drain.

Pour the pasta into the pan with the broccoli, mix well.

Remove red chilli and sprinkle with pepper and a little mozzarella before serving.

SICILIAN SPAGHETTI

Spaghetti with a hearty, colourful sauce boasting a robust flavour.

Serves 4

6 anchovy fillets, chopped
10 g capers
12 big green olives, pitted
500 g tomatoes, peeled and de-seeded if fresh, or sieved if tinned
1 tbsp fresh parsley, finely chopped
1/2 cup basil leaves, finely chopped
1 sprig oregano, finely chopped (or 1/2 tspn dried oregano)
1 tbsp olive oil
2 cloves garlic, finely chopped
Black pepper, freshly ground
500 g spaghetti

Heat the oil in a saucepan and gently cook the garlic and a little black pepper until the garlic is golden.

Add the remaining ingredients.

Bring to the boil then reduce the heat and cover. Cook over a low heat for 20 minutes.

While the sauce is still simmering, cook the spaghetti until *al dente.*

Serve spaghetti topped with sauce.

Accompany with a large green salad and a fresh crusty loaf.

SPAGHETTI MARINARA

A perfect lunch for a summer's day.

Serves 4 to 6

1/2 kg mixed seafood. The best combination is made from prawn flesh, scallops, squid rings, and fish fillets cut into 2 cm squares.

1 tbsp olive oil

3 cloves of garlic, finely chopped

1 cup dry white wine.

1 cup of fish or chicken stock

250 g mussels, or any other molluscs in their shells

Freshly ground black pepper

500 g of spaghetti

2 tbsp chopped parsley

Lightly fry each type of seafood separately in olive oil. They should each take 1 minute. Do not overcook the squid or it will toughen.

Gently cook garlic in pan juices. When soft, add wine and stock. Stir. Cook until the liquor is reduced by half.

While that is happening, start cooking the spaghetti.

Add the mussels to the liquor, cover pan and cook for about 4 minutes. When the mussel shells open, add the cooked seafood. Stir, and simmer very gently. Do not let the fish overcook. Season. The sauce is now ready to serve.

Drain the spaghetti when it is just cooked. Toss the spaghetti with the sauce and seafood, sprinkled with chopped parsley. Serve on a hot dish with fresh bread and a very crisp, dry, white wine.

SUMMERTIME SAUCE

A delicious and colourful vegetable sauce seasoned with anchovies, perfect for serving with plain pasta.

Serves 4

2 red or yellow capsicums, de-seeded and sliced

1 eggplant, peeled and cubed

1 tbsp parsley, finely chopped

12 anchovy fillets, chopped

2 tbsp olive oil

1 small onion, finely sliced

2 cloves of garlic, finely chopped

500 g spiral pasta or fusilli

Heat the oil in a saucepan, add the onion and cook over moderate heat until browned.

Add the capsicum and garlic and cook for 10 minutes, stirring frequently.

Add the eggplant and parsley and cook for a further 10 minutes, stirring frequently.

When the vegetables are cooked add the anchovy fillets and stir the mixture well to distribute them evenly.

Cook a further 1 or 2 minutes.

Serve on a bed of spiral pasta.

MUSHROOM TAGLIATELLE

What makes this dish particularly appealing is the handful of chopped parsley thrown over it before serving.

A flat-leafed variety known as Italian parsley is preferable for this dish as it is more flavoursome than the common curley-leafed variety.

Serves 4 to 6

500 g sliced mushrooms
500 g fresh or dried tagliatelle
2 tbsp olive oil
1 garlic clove, crushed
1 small glass of white wine
1/2 cup chopped parsley
Pepper to taste

Cook the pasta in a large saucepan of boiling water until *al dente*. Drain.

Make the sauce by heating the oil in a frying pan.

Add chopped mushrooms and cook for 2 or 3 minutes.

Add wine and garlic. Simmer gently until the wine has almost evaporated.

Toss the cooked pasta with the mushrooms and parsley.

Season with black pepper.

Serve with a large, fresh, crispy, green salad and fresh crusty Italian loaf.

An Australian chardonnay provides excellent accompaniment.

EGO NOODLES

No, it's not a misprint. Ego noodles is a simple dish of pasta that is so rewarding to prepare that it's good for any cook's ego. It relies for its success on silverbeet, or as it's otherwise known, seakale, Swiss chard or *Beta vulgaris*.

Serves 4

375 g packet egg noodles
1 bunch silverbeet
1 medium onion, chopped
2 cloves garlic, crushed
250 g ricotta
1 tbsp olive oil
1 tspn chilli sauce or sprinkling chilli powder
1/2 tspn grated nutmeg
Black pepper to taste
1 tspn fresh ginger, chopped (optional)
50 g parmesan cheese, grated

Cook pasta in lots of boiling water until *al dente*. Drain.

Strip green leaves from the silverbeet stalks. Wash well and drain. Chop into 2cm strips. Leave on towel to dry. (The stalks may be used in other dishes.)

In large frying pan or wok, gently cook onion, garlic and ginger for 5 minutes.

Increase heat. Add chilli sauce and nutmeg. Stir well.

Stir in silverbeet strips.

Cook over high heat while stirring all the time until silverbeet has softened but still has some bite left in it.

Reduce heat. Mix in noodles and crumble in ricotta.

Toss in parmesan cheese and mix well. Season with black pepper and serve.

CRABBY CHILLI SPAGHETTI

This simple recipe combines crabs and a chilli sauce to make the perfect accompaniment for plain boiled spaghetti. Most crabs are suitable for this dish, however, try to avoid the Japanese giant spider crab which can measure up to 2 metres across the claw tips - impossible to get in the pot. To be certain of freshness, buy crabs live.

Serves 6

3 kg fresh crabs

1 1/2 kg very ripe tomatoes, chopped finely

1 tbsp chilli sauce (chilli-wimps use less)

1 large onion, chopped finely

6 cloves garlic, chopped finely

1/2 bottle white wine (375 ml)

1 tbsp sugar

120 gm jar of anchovies in olive oil (Australian of course)

1 dozen black olives

Freshly ground black pepper

1 packet spaghetti

Freshly grated nutmeg

THE SAUCE

Pour olive oil from anchovies into large pan and gently cook onion and garlic. Add tomatoes, white wine, chilli sauce, anchovies, olives, sugar, freshly ground pepper and simmer slowly until it has reduced to about a third of its original volume.

THE CRABS

Place live crabs in fresh water for 2 or 3 hours to despatch them painlessly.

Pull off the claws and crack with hammer or mallet.

Remove the outer shell from the crabs. Take out conical-shaped gills from under the shell, wash under cold water to flush all sediment and break the body in half lengthways. Wash again to remove any loose shell.

Drain them, but leave them wet. Put the half-bodies and claws in a large saucepan over high heat, with the lid on. Shake well every few seconds for 2 minutes. They will start to steam in the water they were washed in.

Pour sauce over crabs, reduce heat and allow to cook for about 15 minutes, occasionally shaking - but not stirring.

Boil spaghetti in lots of hot water into which nutmeg has been grated until almost cooked, it should still have bite.

Drain spaghetti and toss well with sauce and crabs.

Serve mountains of this mixture to an appreciative audience and include finger bowls of water into which lemon juice has been squeezed.

Rice

Rice is an unassuming but important little grain which does a big job feeding more than a third of the world's population. Worldwide, more than a billion people grow it and Australia plays a big part in producing some of the world's finest rice. In fact, rice growing and processing is one of Australia's unsung export success stories.

Although the cereal has been grown for at least 5,000 years, Australia only began growing it in the nineteenth century. The first success came when farmers in south western New South Wales planted rice between the two great rivers, the Murrumbidgee and the Murray, an area we now know as the Riverina. Since then rice has been springing up in Queensland and in the north of Western Australia, where rice growing was part of the massive Ord River scheme. The Australian industry has grown to such an extent that close to a million tonnes is harvested and processed each year and a massive 90% is exported. It's in such demand that the entire Australian crop is sold each year.

Rice is a great food and we should all eat plenty of it. The National Heart Foundation is right behind it because all plain rice is highly nutritious and low in fat and therefore qualifies for their tick of approval.

But there are still a few of us who worry about cooking rice and are fearful that it'll turn into a gluggy mess. Fear it no more. The new generation of the cereal grown in Australia has come to the rescue.

The following simple recipes are designed to give you the choice of using long grain rice for Asian and Middle Eastern (pilaf or pilau) style dishes, and short grain rice - the type the Italians use in their famous risotto.

BASIC RICE
(Absorption Method)

A simple accompaniment for many of the dishes in this book.

Serves 6 to 8

2 cups long grain rice
2 tspn olive oil
Ground black pepper
Peel of one lemon
2 or 3 spring onions

In a heavy saucepan over heat, toss rice with the oil until it is coated and some of the grains have turned brown.

Put in enough water to cover the rice by about 1 cm. (For a savoury rice, chicken stock may be used.)

Cover and simmer slowly. Check after 15 minutes - if dry add a little more water.

When all the water has been absorbed and the rice is still slightly nutty, it is cooked.

Grate the lemon peel, chop the spring onions and stir them in.

Season to taste and serve with your favourite meat or vegetable dishes.

PILAU STYLE RICE

Serves 4

1 cup rice (washed)
1 tspn oil (I use light olive oil)
1 medium onion
2 or 3 drops of sesame oil
Water (or chicken stock for stronger flavoured rice)

Chop the onion into small pieces and fry in olive oil in a solid pan over high heat until they begin to clarify and brown.

Add the sesame oil and stir in the drained rice.

After a couple of minutes pour in the water or stock to just cover the rice.

Stir well, cover and turn down the heat to very low.

The time it takes depends on the variety of rice you're using. Some of the quick method rice varieties (the ones they say cook in the fridge) take about 20 minutes.

Whatever the rice, no peeking till after 15 minutes, when you can remove the cover to check it.

If there is steam in the pan, there is probably enough water.

If there is no steam and you hear crackling sounds it means the rice has absorbed all the water and is gently toasting on the bottom of the pan.

Just add a little more water.

Check again at 20 minutes. The rice should be just perfect.

A couple of additions to make the rice even tastier and add colour are a few chopped spring onions, the grated zest of a lemon and perhaps a few sesame seeds.

Stir it up well and serve with its garnishes.

I don't add salt. It won't need it, especially if cooked with stock and you are serving it with a tasty savoury dish.

VALUABLE INFORMATION

Throwing rice at weddings originated in India. Rice is a Hindu symbol of fertility. The bride throws three handfuls over the groom, and the groom does the same with the bride. (What a waste!)

PAELLA

One of the world's classic rice dishes comes from Spain - a fabulous mixture of rice, chicken, seafood, vegetables and saffron.

A tasty, visual treat that is easy to prepare.

Its name comes not from the dish itself .but from the pan it is cooked in, a sort of two handled frying pan. However, any large frying pan or electric fry pan will do.

Serves 6 to 8

500 gms skinless chicken leg pieces
250 gms fish fillets
8 raw prawns in shells
12 mussels
1 squid, cleaned
2 cups white rice (short or long grain)
1 large onion
2 capsicums (one red, one green)
Large pinch of saffron strands
1 tbsp chopped garlic
1 cup frozen peas (optional)
4 cups chicken stock
1 bay leaf
1 tbsp olive oil

Partly cook the chicken pieces for a few minutes in a little olive oil. They don't need to be cooked right through at this stage - ten minutes over medium heat should suffice.

Cut the onion into rings, the capsicum into strips, the fish into large cubes and the squid into rings.

Steep the saffron in a couple of tablespoons of boiling water for 5 minutes.

Once the chicken is brown and almost cooked through, toss in the onion, the capsicum and the bay leaf. Cook for 2 minutes. Stir in the squid and cook for 2 minutes.

Add the fish, garlic and the rice and stir up gently. Allow to cook for 2 minutes.

Pour in the stock and saffron liquid. Add water to cover to about 1cm above the rice.

Cover and leave to simmer for 15 minutes over very low heat.

Meanwhile, rinse and drain the prawns and mussels in cold water, discarding any mussels that have opened.

Dot prawns and mussels over the rice mixture. (Frozen peas may be added at this time.)

Cover again and leave to cook slowly for a further 5 minutes to allow mussels, prawns and peas to cook.

Uncover and serve straight from the pan.

SAFFRON

It's the saffron which helps give paella its uniquely Spanish flavour.

It comes from the dried stamen of the mauve, autumn-flowering Crocus sativus.

Hundreds of thousands of flowers must be painstakingly picked and the stamens separated by hand to produce a kilo of saffron, making it the most expensive of spices.

Luckily, only a small pinch of these precious threads is enough to provide the characteristic orange colour and delicate flavour.

Avoid the temptation of using turmeric as a substitute. While appropriate for curries, the flavour just doesn't work with paella.

Sicilian Spaghetti (recipe page 24)

Mushroom Tagliatelle (recipe page 26)

Paella (recipe page 31)

Dolmades (recipe page 34)

Tip: Use meat on the bone when simmering in stock or a sauce - it will remain moist. This is especially so with chicken. Chicken leg pieces are preferable in paella to breast meat, which easily dries out if overcooked.

Tip: If it is all looking too sloppy, put the pan in the oven for a few minutes to dry out, or turn up the heat under the pan. Don't overcook the fish and seafood.

STUFFED TOMATOES

One of Australia's most popular and versatile fruits is the tomato. It is true, strictly speaking the tomato is a fruit, along with the eggplant and capsicum. They are all members of a very large family, the nightshades, which have other relatives which include the potato and tobacco.

The tomato originally came from the Andes but it was not until relatively recently (in the 19th century) that it was regarded as a safe food item.

Until then the English used it as an ornamental plant calling it the love apple.

As well as being an excellent food in its own right, the tomato also makes a great natural container in which to serve other foods. Rice is one of the most popular fillings.

Serves 6 (or 3 piggies)

6 large tomatoes
1 cup rice
2 cloves garlic (finely chopped)
1 large onion, fine;y chopped
1/2 cup each fresh parsley, mint and dill, chopped
2 tbsp tomato pureé
2 tbsp olive oil
1/2 cup lean minced chicken, pork, lamb or beef
1 cup chicken stock
2 tbsp pine nuts
A little grated parmesan or other hard cheese, and fresh breadcrumbs

Cut the top off each tomato where the stalk joins the fruit then remove the centre. Set aside.

In a frying pan, brown rice in a little olive oil. Remove from the pan and set aside.

Fry onions in 1 tbsp olive oil until brown. Add the lean mince and toss in the freshly chopped parsley, garlic, mint and dill.

Stir in half the tomato pureé and the strained juice from the tomatoes.

Add the rice and the chicken or vegetable stock to cover the rice (about 1cm of liquid above the rice).

Turn heat down, cover pan and simmer for 15 to 20 minutes.

While that's cooking, dry the inside of the tomatoes with paper towel.

When the rice is cooked, stir it up and add the pine nuts. Then pack the mixture in the tomatoes.

Make up a mixture of the remaining oil and tomato paste and spoon it over the top.

Place the stuffed fruits onto a lightly oiled baking tray.

Put some vegetables, such as carrots or zucchini, in the spaces, and brush them with a little of the tomato oil mixture.

This will hold the tomatoes upright and prevent them from splitting.

Top with a sprinkling of grated cheese and fresh breadcrumbs.

Finally, put the tray into the oven at 200°C for about 40 minutes.

This mixture can be used for capsicums but they should be boiled in plenty of water for 5 minutes before they're stuffed.

Fact: The high amount of vitamin C in a tomato is found not in the flesh but in the jelly-like substance that surrounds the seeds.

DOLMADES

This classic Greek dish is one of my favourites - tiny parcels of rice and other wonderful ingredients wrapped in vine leaves.

The best I've tasted were made by Melbourne restaurateur Helen Stanogias at the White Village restaurant in Elsternwick.

She agreed to let me in on the secret of how they are made.

Makes 12 dolmades

12 vine leaves
1/2 kg lean mince meat
1 cup raw short grain rice
3 tspn chopped mint
1/2 cup chopped parsley
1/2 cup chopped dill
1 onion finely chopped
20 g canola margarine
1 tspn black pepper
Juice of two lemons

Mix all ingredients except margarine and vine leaves.

If you use fresh vine leaves, blanch them for a few seconds in boiling water. (Well rinsed packet vine leaves are suitable.)

Place vine leaf shiny side down (vein side up) on chopping board. Cut away stem and place a heaped teaspoon of the mixture on stem edge of leaf. Roll up and fold in the sides to make a thick cigar shape. Fill all the remaining leaves.

Load snugly into heavy based pot which has been oiled to stop the parcels from sticking. Put the margarine on top.

Cover parcels with large dinner plate to stop them from floating to the surface during cooking. Pour in water to cover plate. Simmer slowly for about an hour before serving hot or cold.

Traditionally, butter is used in dolmades but margarine has been included here to reduce the amount of saturated fat.

EGGPLANT PILAF

The eggplant - or aubergine - is one of my favourite vegetables. It has such flavour and texture that it makes a perfect replacement for meat in many dishes.

Serves 6

1 large eggplant
Salt for curing eggplant
1 large onion
1/3 cup good olive oil
2 cups chopped, peeled tomatoes or tinned tomatoes
Freshly ground, black pepper
2 tbsp fresh parsley, chopped
2 tspn fresh mint, chopped
2 cups long grain rice
Light stock or water
Low fat natural yoghurt for serving

Slice the eggplants into large cubes, leaving the skin on. Place in a colander and sprinkle with salt. Leave for 30 minutes. Rinse and dry with paper towels.

Cut the onion in half, lengthwise and slice.

Heat 1/2 the oil in a large frying pan (non-stick or enamel if you have one), fry eggplant cubes until lightly browned. Remove from the pan.

Put the remaining oil in the pan and gently fry onion until transparent. Add tomatoes, then pepper, herbs, and finally the fried eggplant. Allow to boil.

Wash the rice thoroughly. Drain and place it in the pan on top of the eggplant mixture. Add stock or water to cover and allow the mixture to boil again, this time without stirring. Reduce heat, cover pan and leave to simmer gently for 30 minutes. Turn off heat, place a cloth over the rim of the pan and replace the lid. Let it stand like this for 10 minutes.

Stir gently and put into a heated serving dish. Serve with low fat natural yoghurt, which may be thickened using the method on page 49.

CHINESE VEGETABLE RICE

Serves 4.

4 cups cold cooked rice
1/2 tspn sugar
1/4 tspn white pepper
6 dried Chinese mushrooms that have been soaked in warm water for 20 minutes then sliced.

1/2 cup celery
1/2 cup green beans
1 cup bean sprouts
2 spring onions, chopped
1/2 cup sliced red capsicum
2 tbsp olive oil
1 tspn sesame oil

Heat both oils in wok or large frying pan. When oil is very hot add mushrooms, onions, celery, capsicum, and beans. Stir fry for about 2 minutes and add sugar and pepper, toss.

Finally add the bean sprouts and rice to vegetables and make sure they are thoroughly mixed together.

Season with a little low salt soy sauce or oyster sauce. Serve immediately.

Salads

In the middle-ages, when I was a boy, 'salad' was another way of saying 'boring'. It amounted to huge chunks of cucumber, slices of beetroot, a few pieces of tomato, and occasionally a radish or two, on a large pile of iceberg lettuce. It was post-war Britain. Forty years later, post-Hawke Australia, and when it comes to salads, most of us are still pretty green.

How often have we been the victim of a 'Greek salad' - four or five black olives, a cube or two of fetta cheese, a few huge chunks of cucumber, on a large pile of iceberg lettuce? Or a salade niçoise - four or five black olives, two lumps of tinned tuna, a hard-boiled egg, on a large pile of iceberg lettuce?

It seems 'salad' can still mean 'boring'. But why? With the wide range of ingredients now within easy reach of most of us there is no excuse for producing something that has the gastronomic appeal of a tray of ice cubes.

Originally salads were the raw leaves of herbs and other plants eaten with a dressing of sal (or salt), hence the name. Although today's lettuces are the basis of a great many salads, it should be noted that a lettuce is mostly water so nutritionally almost any other vegetable will do a better job. I use cresses, beets, spinach, and fresh herbs as much as possible. And when using greens I prefer the cos and buttercrunch lettuces and endives. I strenuously avoid the 'iceberg' - I find it a waste of chewing time and washing water, having no protein, no fibre, and next to no flavour. It's almost as tastless as a real iceberg!

When it comes to a salad it should always be a pleasure to eat.

Thanks to Consuming Passions, it will be.

THE EMPEROR'S NEW SALAD

A member of the pear family, the nashi looks more like an apple although it tastes more like a pear.

The nashi came to Australia from Asia in the mid 1880s when it was introduced by Chinese goldminers.

It has been extensively grown here since the mid 1980s and has found popularity because of its crispness and light refreshing flavour. The main growing centre is in Victoria's Goulburn Valley.

Unlike apples and pears which brown when cut, the nashi discolours slowly, making it perfect in salads. My favourite nashi salad is a variation of the waldorf salad. I call it the Emperor's New Salad as a tribute to the Japanese emperors for whom the nashi was a delicacy.

Makes a big salad, but not quite enough to feed the whole empire!

Lettuce
1 nashi pear
1 cup pecan nuts (or walnuts)
1 cup chopped celery
2 chicken breasts
3 tbsp mayonnaise (see page 76)
1 cup chicken stock
Cherry tomatoes or red capsicum (optional)

Remove skin from chicken breast and poach very gently in chicken stock for about ten minutes until it is just cooked.

Remove from stock and allow to cool. (The stock may be reserved and used in other dishes.)

Cut chicken, celery and nashi into pieces about the size of the nuts and mix with mayonnaise. Add the pecan nuts.

Place on bed of lettuce, garnish with cherry tomatoes or thin strips of red capsicum (optional) and serve with crisp, crusty fresh bread.

And there you have it - a right royal delight.

FIGS AND PROSCIUTTO

This is one of the simplest and most pleasant appetisers or entrées to be served when fresh figs are in season. Prosciutto, being a particularly tasty Italian smoked ham, should not be substituted with a lesser variety.

Serves 6

12 fresh figs
24 black olives
12 very thin slices of prosciutto

Quarter the figs. Place on a large platter with slices of prosciutto and black olives.

If possible, the prosciutto should be sliced in the shop on the day you use it as it dries out very quickly. Even when wrapped in foil and refrigerated it can lose its freshness very quickly.

BASILLED TOMATOES

A good salad to be served alongside a green salad or with hot or cold meat dishes

Serves 4 - 6

500 g tomatoes
Handful fresh basil leaves
Black pepper
1 tbsp wine vinegar
3 tbsp extra virgin olive oil

Slice or dice tomatoes, chop fresh basil leaves and sprinkle over tomatoes. Season with pepper.

Drizzle wine vinegar and olive oil over the salad just before serving.

DEVIL OF A MELON

A novel way of serving a melon is to stuff it with prosciutto and prunes and serve with a light vinaigrette dressing.

Makes a big entrée or even a light meal, depending on the size of your appetite.

Serves 4 to 6

1 large cantaloupe, rockmelon
or honeydew melon
200 g prosciutto ham finely sliced
15-20 good moist prunes, pitted
Juice of 1 lemon
1/2 cup olive oil
1 tspn Dijon mustard

Cut top off melon and remove seeds.

Chop prunes into small pieces. Cut prosciutto into thin strips. Mix well together and fill the melon with the mixture. Replace the lid.

Mix lemon juice, mustard and oil to make a light dressing.

To obtain the maximum effect from this dish, cut the melon into segments at the table. Pour a little dressing over each segment as it is served.

BROCCOLI IN INSALATA
(Broccoli Salad)

Australians have no difficulty buying fresh broccoli at almost any time of the year.

However, in northern Italy, broccoli is a rare and treasured thing. It is considered exotic, because until recently it was virtually impossible to obtain, even though it grew a few hundred kilometres away in the southern regions of the country.

History has it, that the humble vegetable was only ever eaten by northern Italians if they were able to travel to Rome or Naples.

Serves 6

2 bunches broccoli
4 smallish carrots
1/4 cup virgin olive oil
Juice of 4 lemons
1/2 tspn dried chilli flakes (or chilli sauce)
1/2 tspn dried cardamon
Ground black pepper

Put the broccoli into a bowl of ice cold water and leave for half an hour before removing the stalks.

Cut the little florets off the main stems and cut the stalks into strips about 2cm thick and 7cm long.

Put the stalks into a steamer and cook for 5 minutes. Add the florets and cook for a further 4 minutes.

Peel the carrots, then shred them using the peeler. Put the shreds into a bowl of iced water for 5 minutes.

Mix the oil, lemon juice, chilli flakes and pepper in a bowl.

Drain the broccoli and put in a serving dish. Pour half the sauce over the broccoli and mix.

Drain the carrots and then mix them with the rest of the sauce.

Combine them with the broccoli, mix and serve with a sprinkling of cardamon.

WARM CHICKEN SALAD

A touch of Thailand in this simple-to-prepare salad which makes a complete meal.

Serves 4

2 skinned chicken breasts
4-5 spring onions
1 clove garlic, finely chopped
1 red capsicum, finely sliced
100 g unsalted cashews or peanuts
200 g snowpeas
1 tbsp fresh coriander, finely chopped
(or 1/2 tspn dried)
1/2 tspn sesame oil
1 dspn chilli sauce
1 tbsp olive oil
1 tbsp reduced salt soy sauce
Juice of 1 lime (or 1/2 lemon)
Assortment of lettuces

Slice chicken breasts into thin strips.

Marinate in soy sauce, sesame oil and chilli sauce for at least an hour.

Prepare a bed of lettuces on a large serving plate.

Slice spring onions into bite sized pieces.

In large frying pan or wok over very high heat, fry chicken pieces in olive oil for about 1 minute. Do not overcook.

Remove to a warm place.

Stir capsicum, nuts, garlic and snow peas in same pan for a couple of minutes. Toss chicken with other ingredients in the pan.

Serve on lettuce leaves sprinkled with lime juice and fresh coriander.

CAPSICUM CAPER

Serves 4 to 6

1 large ripe tomato

1 clove of garlic, peeled

A few fresh, basil leaves, chopped roughly

15 fresh mint leaves

1/4 cup virgin olive oil

Cracked black pepper

4 large red or yellow capsicums, or a combination of both

2 tbsp capers drained

Cut tomato into pieces. Squash it through a sieve, or even better, use a food mill.

Chop the garlic as finely as you can and add it to the tomato, along with the basil and five of the mint leaves. Pour the oil over the herbs and add pepper. Mix well. Cover and refrigerate for about an hour.

Preheat the oven to 180°C.

Roast the capsicums in the oven by placing them on a shelf with a baking dish of steaming water underneath them. Roast them like this for about 40 minutes, turning them a couple of times so that they are evenly heated.

Remove from oven and put them in a plastic bag. Let them stand for 15 minutes.

Place them in a large bowl of cold water so that their skins come off more easily. Peel, de-seed and de-stem them.

Cut the capsicums into thin strips.

Arrange on a serving dish and pour the dressing over them.

Mix and cover with aluminium foil. Refrigerate for about an hour.

Sprinkle the rest of the mint leaves and capers over them and serve.

THE GRAPE CHICKEN SALAD

Chicken, grapes, capsicums, and mushrooms are the principal players in this salad.

All are available in abundance in Australia and they make a great tasting salad when tossed together.

Serves 8

4 poached skinless chicken breasts
500 g seedless grapes
6 spring onions
1 green capsicum
1 red capsicum
500 g button mushrooms

Cut the chicken into small pieces.

Remove grapes from bunch and wash.

Cut spring onions into julienne (thin lengthwise) strips. Remove seeds and cores from capsicums, cut into julienne strips. Slice mushrooms.

Mix all ingredients in a large serving bowl.

FRENCH MUSTARD DRESSING

1 tbsp Dijon mustard
15 ml white wine vinegar
1 tspn sugar
1 clove of garlic
60 ml extra virgin olive oil
Pepper to taste

Combine dressing ingredients in a bowl and whisk.

Toss through chicken salad.

This salad can be served on its own as a light meal.

SILVERBEET NIÇOISE

The French cheer up the abundant, but perennially dull, silverbeet, like this:

Serves 6

1 bunch of silverbeet
1/2 cup breadcrumbs
2 eggs, beaten
3 or 4 anchovy fillets
1 tspn olive oil
Pepper

Strip the silverbeet leaves from the stalks and wash them in 2 changes of water. Drain and chop into thin strips.

Smear a large saucepan or a wok with the oil and cook the leaves, stirring constantly. There is no need to add water as it will cook in its own juices. When cooked, drain off liquid, chop again very finely.

Mix with breadcrumbs, eggs, finely chopped anchovy fillets and pepper.

Put into shallow baking dish and sprinkle with breadcrumbs. Bake in moderate oven (200°C) for about 20 minutes and it will be ready to serve.

PANZANELLA
(Stale bread salad)

It's true. Stale bread is the basis of this splendid salad from Central Italy. But it must be good bread, such as the bread you make yourself from recipes in this book.

The other ingredients should also be of the highest quality, the freshest vegetables, the richest oil and the finest wine vinegar.

Serves 4-6

4-6 slices of day-old bread

1 small burpless cucumber, peeled and diced

2 or 3 celery sticks (stringless), finely sliced

2 or 3 large salad tomatoes, sliced

1 Spanish onion (best for colour and flavour) finely chopped

1 handful parsley, finely chopped

1 handful basil leaves, chopped

2 cloves finely chopped garlic

DRESSING

4 tbsp extra virgin olive oil

1 tbsp red wine vinegar (preferably balsamic)

Pepper to taste

Soak the bread in cold water for a few minutes. Squeeze out surplus water and crumble bread into a mixing bowl. Add other ingredients and mix thoroughly.

Dress the salad in the Italian way - as opposed to the French way - by drizzling over the oil and vinegar and tossing the salad. Season with pepper. Don't chill this salad as it will lose its flavour, but serve it cool.

SALAD NEARLY NIÇOISE

Serves 6

500 g young stringless beans
500 g potatoes (baby new ones are best but if unavailable cut large ones into manageable pieces)

2 tbsp black olives
1 tbsp capers
3 or 4 anchovy fillets
1 onion
2 tbsp wine vinegar
2 tbsp Dijon mustard
1/3 cup olive oil
Tomatoes
Basil leaves

One of France's most wronged recipes is Salade Niçoise.

We've all experienced the limp lettuce dotted with tinned tuna and beetroot, smeared with sweet commercial dressings masquerading as the genuine article. Even in the 'best' restaurants. Even in Nice!

There seems to be no consensus on what is actually correct.

The former mayor of Nice, Jacques Medecin, who writes cookery books and sues people for libel, maintains that apart from hard-boiled eggs, nothing in a Salade Niçoise should have been cooked.

And that it should contain neither potatoes nor green beans. He may be right.

I offer this version of Salad Nearly Niçoise which I've eaten in Monsieur Medecin's part of the world, and which I prefer to his recipe (genuine or not).

The rule seems to be to include olives, capers, anchovies and tomatoes.

Boil or steam beans until nearly cooked. They should still be crunchy.

Cook potatoes slowly in simmering water. (Potatoes should never be furiously boiled.)

Drain and allow to cool.

Finely chop seeded black olives, capers and anchovy fillets. Slice onion into very thin slices.

Make a dressing by mixing vinegar, mustard and pepper in a bowl then dribbling oil in while stirring all the time till a smooth, creamy consistency is achieved (or shake it all like crazy in a sealed jar).

Toss the vegetables with the olives, capers and anchovy fillets. Stir in the dressing.

Before serving, decorate with pieces of tomato and chopped basil leaves (if available).

NAVEL SALAD

Why not contemplate this bright, refreshing salad which can be served on its own as an appetiser, or with a main course.

Serves 4

6 navel oranges
1 tbsp orange juice, or 1 tspn rosewater
1/8 - 1/4 tspn ground cinnamon, to taste
2 tspn mild-flavoured honey
Pinch freshly grated nutmeg
Garnish: chopped fresh mint

Cut away the skin and pith of the oranges using a small, sharp knife. Hold the oranges over the salad bowl as you do this

so you catch the juice. Slice the oranges into rounds.

Combine the orange juice, or rosewater, cinnamon, and honey and toss with the oranges. Sprinkle with a little nutmeg and chill or serve at once, garnishing with fresh mint.

This salad will keep in the fridge for several hours.

BAKED RICOTTA AND PEAR SALAD

Pears are a marvellous fruit. They can be used in all sorts of dishes - salads, sauces, desserts, and chutneys. Here is a salad which celebrates the adaptability of *Pyrus communis*.

Serves 4 to 6

3 pears
Mixed lettuce leaves
1/4 cup chopped hazelnuts
300 g ricotta cheese
1 tbsp olive oil
Freshly ground black pepper
Juice of 1/2 a lemon

Put the cheese on a baking tray, drizzle with oil and sprinkle with a little pepper.

Bake in a 180°C oven for 35 minutes.

Meanwhile, peel and core pears and cut into slices.

Put them in a bowl of water with the lemon juice.

Remove the cheese from the oven and cut or crumble into small pieces. Drain pears.

Combine the lettuce leaves, pears and cheese.

DRESSING

3 tbsp orange juice
1 tbsp red wine vinegar
2 tspn honey
2 1/2 tbsp olive oil
Small bunch chives, chopped

Whisk ingredients together in a bowl until the honey has dissolved.

Pour over the salad, and gently fold through.

Top with hazelnuts and serve.

HAMATEUR SALAD

A simple salad using cooked potatoes and ham with a few flavours and textures thrown in for good measure.

Serves 4

2 tbsp capers
Sprig parsley
2 or 3 gherkins
250 g lean ham, diced
500 g boiled cooked potatoes, diced
1/2 cup mayonnaise (See page 76)

Chop capers, parsley, gherkins into small pieces.

Mix all ingredients together in a salad bowl with mayonnaise.

POTATO SALAD WITH CUMIN

This potato salad probably originated in North Africa where cumin and potatoes grow plentifully.

We tend to think of potato salads as heavy fillers, however this one is light.

Serves 4

700 g baby potatoes

1/8 to 1/4 tspn harissa (page 75), or cayenne pepper to taste

1 tspn ground cumin

1 tspn olive oil

Juice of 1 large lemon

3 tbsp plain low-fat yoghurt

2 tbsp fresh, chopped coriander, or fresh, chopped parsley

Steam or boil the potatoes until tender (15 to 20 minutes). Wash in chilled water and drain.

Combine the harissa, cumin, olive oil, lemon juice, and yoghurt in a bowl and mix well. Toss with potatoes.

Serve warm or chilled, sprinkled with the fresh coriander.

This potato salad will keep for 2 to 3 days in the fridge as long as you haven't topped with the coriander.

RED QUEEN SALAD

Beautiful, fresh, colourful, surprising, low kilojoule, summer salad.

Serves 4 to 6

1 small red cabbage

1 crisp, tart apple

100 g smoked trout

200 g cottage cheese

2 tbsp low fat yoghurt

2 tbsp chopped parsley

2 tbsp chopped chives

Ground black pepper

Wash and shred the best leaves of the red cabbage.

Peel and cut the apple into small pieces (sprinkle with lemon juice to prevent it going brown).

Mix cottage cheese in a bowl with the yoghurt, parsley, chives and pepper.

Put the cabbage, apple and trout in a serving bowl, sprinkle with the cheese mix. Toss lightly.

Tip: Make it in advance and refrigerate. It benefits from being served really cold.

Devil of a Melon (recipe page 39)

Red Queen Salad (recipe page 48)

Stir Fry Vegetables (recipe page 54)

Artichoke Vinaigrette (recipe page 55)

TZATZIKI

This is a traditional Greek dish. In Greece it is served with very thick full cream yoghurt and lots of garlic. I prefer to use low fat yoghurt, thickened as described below.

Serves 4

4 cups low fat yoghurt
1 long burpless cucumber
3 garlic cloves
Juice of 1/2 lemon
Freshly ground pepper

TO THICKEN YOGHURT

Line a sieve with a linen or cotton tea towel. Pour the yoghurt into it, placing a bowl underneath. Leave in the fridge for 3 hours (excess liquid will be removed).

THE SALAD

Peel the cucumber and slice paper-thin. Let it stand for an hour then wipe with paper towels. Cut the slices into thin julienne strips.

After 3 hours place the yoghurt that has been reserved in the towel into a bowl and whisk until creamy.

Mash the garlic in a mortar and pestle or garlic press until you have a smooth purée. Stir into the yoghurt. Stir in cucumbers and add the lemon juice and pepper to taste.

Serve chilled with hot or cold meat dishes or as a dip with fresh vegetables.

This dish will keep for a day or two in the refrigerator.

IMPERIAL RED SALAD

A delightful salad with more Vitamin C than a bag of oranges and more crunch than an army on parade. Healthy, colourful and goes with meat dishes.

Serves 6 to 8

1/2 red cabbage
1/2 Chinese cabbage
1 red Spanish onion
1 bunch radishes
500 g snow peas
250 g bean sprouts

Shred cabbages. Top and tail peas, then blanch in boiling water. Refresh with cold water. Slice radishes and onion finely. Combine in a salad bowl.

DRESSING

20 ml low salt soy sauce
1 clove garlic, finely chopped
10 ml sesame oil
50 ml olive oil
Juice of 1 lime
Ground black pepper

Combine ingredients in a jar and shake thoroughly. Pour over vegetables and toss.

BEAN THERE, DONE THAT, SALAD

This is a great salad to make if you haven't much time or fresh ingredients.

It makes a complete meal, mostly from tinned foods - the beans and tuna providing protein, carbohydrate and fibre - as well as great flavour.

Serves 4

1 can of white beans
1 large can of tuna in oil
1 red onion, very thinly sliced
2 tbsp red wine vinegar
1 garlic clove, crushed
3 to 4 tbsp fresh basil, chopped
(optional)
1 1/2 tbsp olive oil
1 tbsp plain low fat yoghurt
1 tbsp capers, rinsed
Freshly ground pepper
Garnish: 2 tomatoes cut into wedges
and 1 lettuce

Drain the tuna and the beans. Toss all the ingredients together, adding yoghurt last of all.

Line a bowl with the lettuce leaves, top with the salad, and garnish with the tomato wedges. Serve with fresh Italian bread.

SKINNY ZUCCHINI SALAD

Little gourmet vegetables are very fashionable at the moment. They are used for their aesthetic appeal, as well as their terrific taste.

For little fellows they have such herculean flavours.

Serves 4

500 g small zucchini, washed

1/2 tspn each chilli pepper, powdered cumin, and freshly ground black pepper

4 tbsp chopped parsley

150 ml water

DRESSING

2 tspn good wine vinegar
1 tbsp olive oil
Freshly ground black pepper, as much as you like

Trim ends from zucchini and cut into 5mm thick slices.

Combine the slices in a small saucepan with 150 ml water, chilli pepper, cumin and black pepper.

Cook for a few minutes, or until tender but still crisp. Drain, cool and chill.

Combine dressing ingredients, adding pepper to taste. Add to zucchinis.

Toss well, garnish with chopped parsley, and serve.

RAW-NESSES

Crudités is a dish known to all French people. It is a plate of raw vegetables served as an appetiser. Literally translated, crudité means rawness, hence the name. They're simple to prepare, healthy, cheap, and a lot more interesting than factory produced nibbles.

Serves 6 to 8

100 g snow peas
2 red, yellow or green capsicums
100 g button mushrooms
5 baby zucchini
5 baby carrots
5 tiny turnips
Small bunch of young spring onions
Some My Own 'Naise (page 76), coloured with a little low salt tomato paste.

Top the snowpeas. Core and chop capsicums into rounds. Cut the baby zucchini, carrots, and turnips into halves (lengthways).

Arrange all of the ingredients on a large serving platter.

Serve with of My Own 'Naise.

POTATO MAROC

More than just a potato salad; the Moroccans perform miracles with the humble spud.

Serves 4-6

1 kg potatoes
A little grapeseed oil

DRESSING

4 tbsp virgin olive oil
1 1/2 tbsp vinegar
2 tbsp finely grated onion
2 tbsp finely chopped flat-leafed parsley
1/4 tspn paprika
1/4 tspn chilli powder
Freshly ground black pepper

Cook the potatoes in their skins in boiling water until just tender.

Drain and peel while still hot.

Brush with grapeseed oil and allow to cool. When cold, dice.

Mix all the dressing ingredients in a small bowl. Toss with potatoes and chill.

ANCHOVY DIP

A light fish dip to have with crisp fresh salad vegetables.

I always use Australian anchovies in olive oil - they are lower in salt than the imported variety.

Makes a bowl of dip!

1 cup low fat natural yogurt
1 small red onion, finely chopped
10 anchovy fillets in olive oil
2 tbsp parlsey, chopped
1 clove garlic, crushed
Juice and rind of 1 lime (or 1/2 lemon)
1/2 tsp freshly ground black pepper
150 g day old white bread minus their crusts

Blend all ingredients except the bread.

Slowly add bread until desired consistency is reached. Chill before serving.

Vegetables

There is an old saying that the English have three vegetables, two of which are cabbage. And when I grew up in England that seemed almost to be the case. I remember potatoes, peas, carrots, cabbage and not much else. Most of it was boiled to a pulp.

Nowadays, the range of vegetables available to most of us is fantastic. As a result of refrigerated transport, however, most varieties are available all year round, which means that we are buying expensive overseas produce out of season, rather than waiting to eat locally grown vegetables when they are at their best. And cheapest.

As well as being beautiful to eat, vegetables generally are low in fat, high in fibre and rich in vitamins.

When buying vegetables, look for the local-grown. The colour should be bright and the vegetable firm. Avoid those which show evidence of old age - wilted leaves and discoloration - and those which are gigantic - their growth was probably forced and they may be tasteless.

Root vegetables are best stored at cool temperatures - ideally not more than 15°C. Soft, leafy vegetables, such as lettuces, should be stored loosely wrapped in the crisper compartment of the refrigerator. Store vegetables away from fruit and do not wash them until just before you prepare them for cooking or eating. Moisture can hasten the rotting process and may leach out vitamins.

Much of a vegetable's flavour and goodness may be near the surface so it's a good idea where possible to eat the skin.

Certain vegetables contain bitter juices which should be removed before cooking.

Most notable is the eggplant, which should be sliced, sprinkled with salt and left to stand for at least 30 minutes. Then rinse well to remove the salt and bitterness, and dry with paper towel before cooking.

Other vegetables, which are no longer as young as they would like to be, might also need to go through this process: zucchini and cucumbers, for instance.

Some vegetables benefit from blanching which removes any very strong flavours. This process of plunging them into boiling water for a few moments also prevents discolouring. After blanching, vegetables may be kept overnight in the refrigerator.

Two important rules for cooking vegetables: do not overcook and never salt the cooking water. Any seasoning should be done just before serving.

STIR FRYING

Most vegetables are suitable for stir frying, which keeps them looking and tasting great.

Wash, drain and cut them into strips or short pieces. Heat 1 tspn sesame oil in a hot wok over a fierce heat. Throw in vegetables, stirring constantly. Sprinkle in a few drops of sherry and reduced salt soy sauce. Add 1/2 tspn chilli sauce for added zing.

They should be cooked for about 3 minutes.

THE GOOD OIL ON OLIVE OIL

There is a range of olive oils available from extra light to extra virgin.

Basically, the extra virgin is the first pressing of the olive. It may also be labelled 'cold pressed'. It has a low acidity and a stronger flavour than the more refined oils making it great for salads and salad dressings.

A middle range oil, which may be labelled 'pure', is usually a blend with a less assertive olive flavour and may be used for salads or cooking.

The extra light olive oil is ideal for cooking, where you do not want the overpowering flavour of the fruit.

Whether you use extra virgin or extra light, remember that oil is fat so it is a good idea to use it in moderation.

ARTICHOKE VINAIGRETTE

Fresh artichokes are a wonderful springtime treat, especially when cooked simply and served warm with a lemon vinaigrette dressing.

Serves 4

4 artichokes
2 lemons
1/3 cup virgin olive oil
2 tspn smooth Dijon mustard
1 tspn black pepper

Rinse artichokes well in cold water. Chop off the stalks and pop them into a pan of boiling water. Squeeze in the juice of a lemon and for added flavour drop in the peel as well.

Put a plate on top of the artichokes to keep them under the water and boil for 40 minutes.

While they are cooking, make the dressing by mixing the olive oil with the mustard, pepper and the juice of the other lemon.

Stir it up well and that's it. To see if the artichokes are cooked, pierce the base with a fork. It should be soft. Leave them to drain upside down for a few minutes then pour over the dressing.

To eat, just pull out a leaf at a time and suck the fleshy part at the base. When you've enjoyed this experience, you'll find the succulent heart of the vegetable waiting for you. I remove the furry choke before eating the heart.

Tip: Artichokes should be bought with a good firm head. Squeeze the vegetable gently before you buy. It won't mind, although the storekeeper might.

RATATATOUILLE

The joy of cooking vegetables when they are in season makes for tasty, colourful combinations. This dish is simple and delicious.

I call it RATATATOUILLE since it is based on the classic French Mediterranean dish, ratatouille, but has a little more going for it, a little more "tatat".

The secret is the addition of good Australian rice.

There are no hard and fast rules about vegetables.

You may use what you like in whatever proportions you like but I avoid using root vegetables.

Serves 6 to 8

3 cups cooked rice, white or brown, long or short grain

1 medium sized eggplant

1 large onion

3 or 4 cloves garlic

2 capsicums (one red, one green)

1/2 red cabbage

1 large zucchini

2 or 3 tomatoes

2 tbsp extra virgin olive oil

2 tbsp fresh oregano chopped finely

A few leaves basil chopped finely

Cut all the vegetables into similar bite-sized pieces.

Toss the eggplant pieces in salt and allow to stand for 30 minutes to get rid of any bitter juices.

Wash well, drain and dry with paper towel.

Crush the peeled garlic and chop it up

with some fresh oregano. If I can't get fresh oregano I use the tiniest amount of dried. But it should not be allowed to overpower the subtle vegetable flavours.

I leave the basil until later because being a much more delicate leaf than oregano, it bruises and is best left until the last minute.

Heat 2 tbsp of oil in a large pan. Add the onions and eggplant. Cook for 5 minutes.

Then add the capsicum and cook for 2 or 3 minutes. Stir in the zucchini. Add the garlic, cabbage and oregano. Stir.

Finally, add the tomatoes and basil, which should be just warmed through. Cover and simmer for a few minutes. Not too long - the vegetables should still have some crunch in them.

Add some black pepper and stir in the rice. Garnish with fresh basil and it is ready to serve hot or cold.

Fact: Cabbage is a member of the oldest of vegetable families, the brassicas. Its relatives include mustard. When it's included in this dish it does give a slight mustardy flavour.

AUBERGINE PROVENÇALE

I enjoyed this marvellously simple dish at Chez Antoine Restaurant in Aix-en-Provence.

It is run by a third generation French/Italian family of cooks who believe in using the freshest local ingredients cooked simply in styles more commonly found in Italy than in France.

This dish makes an ideal entrée, or it can be served with plain spaghetti as a main meal.

Serves 4 to 6

1 large eggplant

250 g tomato sauce (See page 74)

100 g grated fresh reduced fat mozzarella or boccancini

Fresh thyme, oregano or basil

Olive oil to cook eggplant

100 g plain flour

Parmesan cheese to garnish

Slice aubergine, salt and allow to stand for half an hour to remove bitter juices.

Wash, dry and dust with seasoned flour before frying in a little olive oil for 4 or 5 minutes until they are browned.

In the bottom of a ceramic or glass baking dish spread some tomato sauce, lay a carpet of aubergine pieces, then more sauce, and a sprinkling of the grated cheese and fresh herbs.

Repeat the operation until all of the aubergine has been used, finishing with tomato sauce topped with a little parmesan.

Bake in oven at 190°C for 40 minutes.

Serve hot or cold with crusty fresh bread and a big green salad.

Since eggplant is inclined to be a bit oil thirsty, it's a good idea to use a non-stick pan to reduce the amount of oil necessary for this dish.

CABBAGE ROLLS

Wonderful parcels of nutrition containing herbs, lots of nuts, plenty of vegetables, and no oil.

Serves 6

12 small or 6 large cabbage leaves
5 spring onions, finely chopped
2 cups of cooked rice
1 grated carrot
1 tbsp chopped dill
1/2 cup pine nuts, toasted in dry pan
1/2 cup currants
2 tbsp tomato paste
1 large garlic clove, finely chopped
1 tbsp chopped mint
1 cup chicken stock
1 tspn sugar
Freshly ground black pepper

Preheat oven to 180°C.

Carefully cut away the stalky centre rib of each cabbage leaf.

Soften the leaves with boiling water. If they are large leaves, cut them in half; if small, overlap where their ribs have been removed.

Mix the spring onions, rice, carrot, dill, pine nuts and currants together.

Divide the filling evenly and place on individual leaves. Roll each leaf tightly together like a parcel and arrange them, seam-side down, on a greased, ovenproof dish.

Combine the rest of the ingredients and pour over the cabbage rolls. Cover, and bake in the oven for 40 minutes.

Tip: If the rolls look as though they are drying out, add a little water.

BRAISED FENNEL

Fennel is a tall herb with feathery foliage and an aniseed flavour which grows as a weed in parts of Australia.

It has been used for centuries to treat digestive complaints and chewing the seeds is said to allay hunger.

The bulbous base of the stem may be sliced and either eaten raw or cooked, as in this recipe.

Serves 4

1 fennel bulb
1 tbsp olive oil
2 tbsp water
Black pepper

Peel and slice the fennel bulb as you would an onion. Remove the tough centre pieces.

Fry it gently in the olive oil for a minute or so, until all the rings break up and are coated.

Add water. Now put a lid on the pan and continue cooking over low heat until tender. This should take about 15 minutes.

Remove lid, season with pepper, then increase heat and toss the fennel until most of the liquid has evaporated.

Braised Fennel is delicious served with fish.

STIR FRY CABBAGE

Cabbage in my youth, meant sloppy, over-cooked dollops of tasteless, green stuff served at school.

It took a couple of decades to rid myself of my aversion to it.

Now I appreciate the vegetable and you will too if you try this recipe.

It preserves the integrity of this fine, upstanding member of the Brassica family.

Serves 4 to 6

1 cabbage
1 tbsp olive oil
1/2 tspn sesame oil (optional)
100 g lean bacon
1 tspn mustard seeds
1/2 tspn black pepper
1/2 tspn nutmeg, grated

Cut the cabbage into thin slices.

Heat the oil in a large frying pan or wok.

Toss in the cabbage and bacon and keep on tossing for about 5 or 6 minutes until it becomes tender but still crunchy.

Stir in the mustard seeds, nutmeg and black pepper. Serve steaming hot.

SPICY ITALIAN-STYLE CAULIFLOWER

This makes a change to plain, steamed cauliflower.

It takes only a few more minutes to prepare and goes superbly with most meat dishes.

Serves 4 to 6

1 whole cauliflower, broken into florets
1 tbsp virgin olive oil
3 garlic cloves, minced
1 tspn chilli sauce
2 tbsp white wine
Freshly ground pepper

Steam the cauliflower for 10 minutes or until tender but still firm. Drain.

Heat the olive oil over medium heat in a non-stick pan and sauté the garlic for 1 minute.

Add the chilli sauce, then the cauliflower and wine. Sauté, stirring for 3 to 5 minutes.

Add pepper to taste and a few strips of red capsicum for colour, if desired. Serve immediately.

PILAKI

The Turkish way to cook vegetables and make a salad dressing at the same time.

Serves 4

1 large onion, sliced
3 garlic cloves, crushed
3 large tomatoes, chopped
5 different coloured capsicums, sliced
1 tbsp olive oil
1 tspn ground cumin
1/4 tspn cayenne pepper
1 cup water
Freshly ground pepper
Juice of 1 lemon
1 tbsp fresh parsley, chopped
1 tbsp fresh mint or basil, chopped

Heat the oil over a medium heat in a large frying pan (preferably non-stick), add onions and garlic.

Sauté for a few minutes, until the onions begin to soften, then add tomatoes, capsicum, and cumin.

Continue cooking for about 5 minutes, stirring continuously. Stir in the cayenne and water and bring to a simmer.

Reduce the heat and simmer the vegetables, uncovered for about 15 minutes or until the water has evaporated, stirring every now and then.

Season to taste with pepper, then remove from heat.

Allow to cool, then cover and chill.

Just before serving, stir in the lemon juice and parsley. Garnish with mint or basil.

This salad will keep for a day or two in the fridge as long as you don't include the lemon juice and parsley before refrigerating.

NAKED CHILDREN IN THE GRASS

A Belgian delight with a delightful name.

Serves 4

500 g dried lima beans or other small dried beans

4 cups water

750 g stringless green beans

2 tspn virgin olive oil

2 tspn sugar

Soak the beans overnight in water. Then bring to the boil and cook for 45 minutes.

Cut the green beans into 3 cm pieces. Add the lima beans and simmer over a relatively low heat for another 15 minutes.

Drain, transfer to a warm serving dish and stir in oil and sugar. Serve with any meat dish.

PROVENÇALE TOMATOES

Ideal accompaniment to savoury dishes that do not contain tomatoes.

Serves 4

5 or 6 small salad tomatoes

2 tbsp olive oil

1 clove garlic, finely chopped

Sprig of parsley, finely chopped

2 or 3 tbsp breadcrumbs

A few leaves of thyme or basil, or 1/2 tspn of either dried herb

Pepper

Wash tomatoes, cut them in half horizontally and scoop out seeds. Fry quickly in olive oil, scorching the top and bottom. Put upright in baking dish.

Fill and cover with a mixture of garlic, parsley, breadcrumbs, thyme, and basil. Season with pepper and bake in moderate oven for about 10 minute. Serve hot.

GREEK-STYLE MUSHROOMS

Mushrooms are a good source of B-group vitamins. Look for field mushrooms, they have better flavour than the cultivated variety.

Serves 4 to 6

250 g fresh mushrooms
500 g of fresh tomatoes, peeled
1 chopped onion
1 tbsp olive oil
1 glass of dry white wine
Juice of 1/2 a lemon
1 tbsp of tomato concentrate
1 bay leaf
1 sprig thyme
Pepper

Wipe the mushrooms clean, or wash them if they are sandy. Cut them into quarters or if they are the field variety 2 cm pieces.

Stew the tomatoes in olive oil with the chopped onion, wine, lemon juice, and tomato concentrate. Reduce to a thick sauce. Add mushrooms, bay leaf, thyme, and pepper. Simmer till mushrooms are cooked (about 15 minutes). Refrigerate. Serve chilled.

This dish is particularly tasty if it is made the day before serving.

MUSHROOMS

Mushrooms were enjoyed as long ago as 3000 BC, but they have only been cultivated during the last three centuries. Cultivated mushrooms are sold in three sizes: buttons - small, unopened immature mushrooms; cups or caps are larger, but still with rounded caps; and flats - open mushrooms with a stronger flavour.

Buy dry, undamaged ones. Store in a paper bag in a cool dark place. Clean before use by shaking in a clean tea towel.

Eat them raw, cooked or marinated for a couple of hours in a mixture of olive oil and lemon juice.

Soups and Sauces

When I was a boy I spent some time in Belgium, where there were two take-away foods: chips and soup. The chips were served much as they are today, in paper cones with a dollop of homemade mayonnaise. The soups were also homemade.

My mother would send me with a tureen and 20 francs to collect the 'potage' from 'madame' who lived just down our street. It was a rich brew usually of vegetables, potato, leek and onions, along with several handfuls of chopped chervil, a herb which gave the potion its characteristic slightly aniseed and peppery flavour.

Homemade soups were very much part of Belgian culture, much as they have been throughout most of Europe, where the simmering of vegetables, herbs, meat and bones has also been the basis of stocks and sauces.

Most soups and sauces begin as stock - or bouillon, in France. The main advantage in making your own is that you can ensure that the fat and salt contents are kept to a minimum.

There are four basic stocks: white, brown, fish and vegetable. White stock is made using veal bones and vegetables such as onion, leek, celery and carrot, which are simmered uncovered in a pot for a couple of hours or more. Brown stock is also made using veal or beef bones but which have been browned in a hot oven. This not only colours the bones but also allows fat to drain off. Additionally, tomatoes are often used to add further colour to brown stock.

Chicken bones may also be used to make stock but should only cook for up to an hour. Prolonged cooking causes chicken stock to become bitter.

Herbs and garlic may be added to the stock. The herbs I use are thyme, bay leaf and oregano or marjoram.

Making your own fish stock is a smelly business. There are commercial fish stocks which serve most purposes. I also frequently opt for chicken stock in fish dishes, its flavour is less obvious.

Once cooked, the stocks should be strained and allowed to chill in the refrigerator. When cold, a layer of fat will form on the surface. This may be removed.

The stock may then be reduced to concentrate its flavour. Simply put back on the heat. Remove any remaining fat by drawing a piece of paper towel across the surface.

There may still be some cloudiness remaining in the liquid. This is not a problem if using the stock in thick soups or sauces. However, if making a consommé, the stock can be clarified by stirring beaten egg whites into it as it is warming up.

Once it starts to boil, stop stirring, turn down the heat and allow to simmer for about 1/2 hour. A scum of cooked egg white containing remaining particles will form on the surface. Strain it off to leave a perfectly clear golden consommé.

TRIED AT FREDS

LENTIL AND CORIANDER SOUP

A Moroccan-style soup using kasbour, or as it is commonly known, coriander. This herb is used in practically all cooking in Morocco. I use Vietnamese mint when coriander is scarce.

Serves 6

450 g shin of veal

100 g lentils

3 tbsp olive oil

1 1/2 Spanish onions, peeled and coarsely grated

1/4 tspn each crushed black pepper and chilli powder

Water

2 large potatoes, peeled and diced

2 large carrots, peeled and sliced

1 bunch fresh coriander, coarsely chopped

Lemon juice

Pour boiling water over lentils, let them soak for 15 minutes, then rinse and drain.

While they are soaking, put oil, veal, onion, black pepper and chilli powder, in a large flameproof casserole, stirring all

Pistou Resistance (recipe page 65)

Mean Green Soup (recipe page 69)

Grapefruit Dressing (recipe page 77)

Fish with Pawpaw Sauce (recipe page 82)

the time until the onion becomes transparent. Add 1.5 litres of water and bring to the boil.

Add lentils and cook for 1 1/2 hours. Top up water occasionally if necessary.

After an hour and 10 minutes, add potatoes and carrots. Simmer until the vegetables are tender. Stir in coriander and lemon juice and serve at once.

> *Never throw left-over fresh coriander away. Although a fragile herb, it can be kept in the refrigerator in a glass of water for at least a week.*

PISTOU RESISTANCE

The French call this a soup. They are being unduly modest. Pistou is a supercharged gastronomic scene stealer.

It is a triumph not just because it is a great vegetable soup, but because it's served with a mixture which gives it its name, a delicious sauce of basil, garlic and olive oil. It is within reach of those of us who are able to acquire fresh basil. For the rest of you - I'm deeply sorry.

If you plan to serve it as an entrée, you'll only need a very light main course, perhaps a grilled sardine on a lettuce leaf.

Serves 8

THE SOUP

2 large onions, sliced into rings

2 leeks, sliced into rings

2 sticks celery, diced

2 large potatoes, cubed

2 carrots, sliced

200 g fresh green beans, chopped into bite size pieces

200 g dried beans (haricot, kidney etc.)

5 or 6 cloves garlic crushed

2 tbsp extra virgin olive oil

200 g cooked macaroni

2 litres water (approx.)

The day before, soak the dried beans in cold water.

Using a heavy saucepan or stockpot, gently cook the onions, leeks, carrots and celery for 5 minutes in the olive oil. Add soaked dried beans, green beans, potato pieces and garlic. Cover with water and simmer for 1 1/2 hours.

Just before serving, season to taste and stir in the macaroni.

THE PISTOU SAUCE

3 cloves garlic, finely chopped
1 cup chopped fresh basil
1/2 cup olive oil
1 egg yolk
Parmesan cheese

Pound the fresh basil and garlic in a mortar - or blender. Add egg yolk.

Gradually stir in the olive oil, starting a few drops at a time - as you would a mayonnaise. The mixture should thicken.

To serve, put a small dollop of sauce in each warmed bowl and a sprinkle of parmesan cheese.

Then pour on a good amount of soup and ask everyone to wait a full 2 minutes, savouring the wonderful aroma, before stirring the mixture up well and eating with tremendous enthusiasm.

Truly, this is one of the world's great dishes.

Note: The pistou sauce will go brown if exposed for a long time to air. It sort of rusts. This is not a problem, except that it can look unsightly. The solutions are either to put it in an airtight jar and cover with a thin layer of olive oil or to make up the sauce immediately before serving. The sauce will keep in the refrigerator for several days.

PEA SUPER

This Venetian soup recipe was originally made with rice. The rice version is delicious but this one is more of a broth than a thick soup.

Serves 4

250 g pasta (shell or spiral)
300 g fresh peas, shelled
50 g bacon, fat removed
1 1/2 cups beef broth or stock
(See Beef Broth on page 74)
500 g tomatoes, peeled and de-seeded,
or sieved if tinned

Freshly ground black pepper
2 tbsp olive oil
2 cloves garlic, crushed
1 small onion, finely chopped
Fresh basil leaves, finely chopped

Heat the oil in a large pot. Add the onion, garlic and basil.

Fry until the onion and garlic are pale brown. Add the peas and bacon, stirring well.

Pour in the broth, the tomatoes and pepper. Bring to the boil, cover and simmer for 15 minutes.

Return to the boil then add pasta. Cook until *al dente*.

Serve at once with crusty wholemeal bread - a meal in itself.

PROVENÇALE FISH SOUP

A simple fish soup which may be made with just about any type of firm-fleshed fish.

I like to use a mixture of small and large fish such as trevally, mullet, sardines and snapper.

I also include fish heads, which are removed before serving. They are a great source of flavour.

Serves 6 to 8

2 kg fish cut into large pieces
1/2 litre chicken or fish stock
1 large onion cut into slices
1 leek cut into rings
1 carrot cut into strips
2 medium tomatoes
2 or 3 cloves of garlic, crushed
1/2 cup chopped parsley
1 tbsp chopped, fresh thyme,
oregano or fennel
Juice of 1/2 a lemon
2 or 3 strips of lemon peel
1 dspn cornflour
1 tbsp olive oil
1 tspn pepper

In a large, heavy bottomed pot, cook the vegetables and garlic in a little olive oil.

When they have softened add herbs, lemon juice and peel. Stir. Add fish pieces, and chicken or fish stock.

Cover with water and simmer very gently for 40 minutes. Do not stir during this time.

Very gently, strain mixture. Put strained liquor back into pot and reduce over medium heat.

Sort the good pieces of fish flesh from the bones. Throw away the heads and bones, keeping only the flesh.

Now take the liquor off the heat. Mix cornflour with 1 tablespoon of cooled liquor and pour back into the pot to thicken the mixture.

Return fish to liquor, season with black pepper and serve with a fresh, crusty wholemeal loaf - ideal for dunking in this wonderful soup.

FAT WEEVIL SOUP

Fat weevil soup or, as it should be called, Barley Broth, is an oldie but a goodie. It is perfect for warding off winter chills. Barley is an excellent source of fibre. I feel it really should be eaten wearing a tartan dressing gown.

Serves 6

3 lamb shanks
2 carrots, 1 parsnip, 1 turnip,
2 onions and 2 sticks celery
White pepper
1/4 - 1/2 packet barley

Wash and grate carrot, parsnip and turnip. Chop onion and celery.

Place all ingredients into a large pot and just cover with water.

Add white pepper to taste. Bring to the boil and then simmer for 3 hours.

Serve with fresh bread.

KASHMIRI TOMATO SOUP

Cardamon and cumin give this marvellous soup its Kashmiri character. Though I use ten cardamon pods, if it's a spice that's new to you, use two or three only.

Serves 4

450 g fresh tomatoes
6 cups cold water
1 large onion, finely chopped
1 tbsp olive oil
1 tbsp wholemeal flour
1 tbsp tomato pureé
10 cardamom pods, crushed in pestle and mortar
2 1/2 cm piece of cinnamon stick
Freshly ground black pepper
Fresh mint to garnish

Simmer the tomatoes in water for 10 minutes, stirring occasionally.

Meanwhile, fry the onion in the oil until it has softened, about 5 minutes.

Add the onion to the tomatoes.

Mix the wholemeal flour to a paste with a little of the remaining liquid, then add this to the tomatoes.

Add the rest of the ingredients.

Simmer uncovered for 15 minutes.

Adjust the seasoning to taste.

Strain the mixture through a sieve, forcing it through with the back of a spoon, then reheat and pour into bowls.

Serve topped with a spoonful of yoghurt and sprinkled with mint leaves.

MEAN GREEN SOUP

A lovely aromatic, bright green soup. This one is a feast for all the senses (except hearing - it is perfectly quiet).

Serves 4 to 6

1 kg leeks, white part only
2 tbsp olive oil
Freshly ground black pepper
1 squeeze fresh lemon juice
1 cup spinach leaves, well washed
1 cup green peas
1 cup shredded lettuce
5 cups water
1 tbsp finely chopped fresh parsley
1 tbsp finely chopped fresh basil

Cut leeks in half lengthwise, and run cold water over them. Pat dry and cut into thick slices.

Warm olive oil over low heat in a heavy-bottomed soup pot. Add leeks. Add a little pepper and lemon juice, cover and cook over a low heat for 20 minutes, stirring often.

Add other vegetables, stir for a couple of minutes, then add the water. Bring to boil, reduce heat, cover and simmer until they are thoroughly tender (5 to 10 minutes). Just before serving, add more pepper and stir in the herbs.

This soup can be refrigerated for a day or two.

TOMATO BASIL FAULTLESS

A foolproof tomato and basil soup. To be served hot in winter and cold in summer. Sybil would love it!

Serves 4 to 6

1 kg tomatoes, peeled and chopped
3 cups chicken stock (see page 73)
1 small onion, chopped
5 cloves of garlic, crushed
1 tbsp olive oil
Freshly ground pepper
Handful of basil leaves
Juice of 1/2 lemon (for chilled version)
Sprinkling of fresh basil for garnish

Heat the oil in a large soup pot and add the onion and half the garlic. Cook gently over medium heat for about 5 minutes.

Add the tomatoes and remaining garlic. Cook for about 10 minutes, stirring often.

Add the chicken stock, the basil leaves, then the pepper to taste, bringing to a simmer. Cover and simmer for 30 minutes.

Remove from the heat and pureé in a food processor. If serving hot, ladle into bowls.

If serving cold, refrigerate until thoroughly chilled. Just before serving, stir in the lemon juice and a little more pepper to taste. Serve garnished with the additional basil.

This soup will keep in the refrigerator for a couple of days and is terrific chilled.

PROVENÇALE GARLIC SOUP

If the old wives' tale is true about garlic preventing colds, you'd be fully protected if you ate a bowl of this every day.

Serves 4

4 cups chicken stock
6 large garlic cloves, minced
1 tspn fresh thyme
4 fresh sage leaves, chopped,
or 1/2 tspn dried
1 bay leaf
1 egg yolk
2 tbsp chopped, fresh parsley

Bring the water to the boil, then add the

garlic, thyme, sage, and bay leaf. Simmer for 10 to 15 minutes. Remove bay leaf.

Next beat the egg yolk in a bowl and slowly ladle in some hot soup. Stir, then return to the soup and combine.

Serve at once, topping each bowl with parsley.

SNOWPEA SOUP ...like this Pea Soup!

A soup that is neither too heavy, nor too light.

It can be served chilled during summer as a refreshing appetiser, or hot in winter as an alternative to heavier soups that leave little room for main courses.

Serves 4

1 tbsp olive oil
3 spring onions, chopped
350 g snowpeas
1 medium potato, chopped
4 cups chicken stock
1 tbsp fresh coriander, chopped
2 tbsp low fat yoghurt

Heat the oil in a saucepan, add spring onions. Stir over a medium heat for about 2 minutes or until they are soft. Top the snowpeas and add them with potato and stock to the pan.

Bring to boil, reduce heat, cover and simmer for about 10 minutes or until peas are just soft.

Blend or process the mixture until smooth. Return to the saucepan, bring to the boil, and remove from heat. Stir in coriander and yoghurt.

> *Australians call them snowpeas. Britons call them mange tout, which comes from the French. But the French call them haricots plats which in English means flat beans!*

SOUP SON

I include this potato soup recipe not for any sentimental reason connected with my possible ancestor Auguste Antoine Parmentier, who made culinary history in France with his potato recipes, but because it is a thoroughly good winter soup.

Serves 4

2 large onions, sliced
4 rashers lean bacon, finely chopped
1 tbsp olive oil
1 tbsp plain flour
4 cups chicken stock
1 cup dry white wine
2 tbsp chopped parsley
Freshly ground black pepper
500 g potatoes, peeled and sliced
1 cup low fat yoghurt
2 egg yolks
1 extra tbsp parsley

Sauté onions and bacon in a little olive oil. When onions have softened, sprinkle with flour and cook for a further minute.

Add stock, a little at a time, stirring continuously over low heat.

Add the wine and cook for a further couple of minutes. Add parsley, pepper and the potatoes.

Simmer gently until potatoes are cooked (about 15 minutes), stirring occasionally.

Mix together yoghurt and egg yolks. Stir into the soup, simmer for further 2 minutes. Do not allow to boil.

Serve soup garnished with a sprinkle of parsley and a crusty loaf of French bread - excellent for dunking. Bon appetit!

WHOLE MEAL SOUP

A wonderfully hearty whole meal, prepared very simply.

Serves 4-6

1 kg well washed spinach or silverbeet, chopped

2 tbsp olive oil
2 cloves garlic, crushed
Freshly ground black pepper
6 cups chicken stock
1/2 cup rice
Parmesan cheese to garnish

Wash and cook spinach in the small amount of water remaining on the leaves. When cooked, squeeze out as much liquid as possible. Set aside.

In a large pot heat oil and add garlic. Cook for a couple of minutes making sure it doesn't brown. Add spinach, stock and pepper. Bring the soup to the boil and add rice, stir frequently for about 20 minutes or until the rice is done.

Serve in individual bowls and sprinkle with a little parmesan.

HOMEMADE STOCK

Makes up to 2 litres

2 kgs stock bones or chicken carcasses
2 carrots
2 onions
2 leeks
2 celery sticks
A couple of bay leaves
Fresh thyme and/or rosemary
Black pepper
Water to cover

Put bones in a large pot, cover with water and bring to the boil.

Turn down heat and allow to simmer in near boiling water. Remove scum from top of water.

When no more scum is forming, add vegetables, herbs and pepper and continue simmering for 2 or 3 hours. (I sometimes use a pressure cooker if using just chicken carcasses because they tend to have less waste material to skim.)

Strain and put liquor back into pot. Slowly reduce over low heat until a third of the original amount remains.

Pour into dish, cover, and when cool, put in the fridge.

The next day, skim off the solidified fat. The stock is now ready to use, either in soup or as a basis for a sauce. If you wish to keep it in a more concentrated form, reduce it further over a low heat until it is a syrup and then freeze.

CHICKEN BROTH
(or STOCK)

This recipe makes an Asian-style broth which can be served on its own or used as a delicious stock, and you can use the chicken flesh for other dishes.

Serves 6 as a soup

1 whole chicken
1 tspn fresh ginger
3 spring onions
1 tspn sesame oil

Bruise the ginger with the back of a knife and place it with the spring onion inside the chicken.

Rub sesame oil all over the outside of the chicken and place in a large stock pot. Cover with water. Bring to the boil, turn down heat and cook for 30 minutes.

Turn off the heat and let the chicken stand in the stock for 45 minutes before removing it.

Strain broth, allow to cool and refrigerate. When fat has solidified remove from surface.

Reheat broth and serve with thin slices of chicken and chopped spring onions.

BEEF BROTH OR STOCK

A tomato flavoured broth that can be served on its own or used as a base for other soups.

You can use any beef or veal bones or pieces of meat for this recipe.

I prefer marrow bone from the leg.

Serve 6 as a soup

1 carrot, chopped
1 onion, peeled and quartered
1 stalk celery, chopped
1 green capsicum, chopped
425 g can tomatoes
2 potatoes, chopped
2-3kg beef bones

Place all the ingredients in a large stock pot and cover with water.

Bring to the boil. Reduce heat to simmer. Place a lid half on the pot. Every now and then, skim away any froth.

Cook for 3 hours over a very low heat - don't let it boil.

Strain broth, allow to cool and refrigerate. When fat has solidified remove from surface.

TWICE THE SPICE TOMATO SAUCE

An excellent sauce that can be used with pasta or as an accompaniment to barbecued meats.

Serves 6

1 kg fresh, juicy, peeled tomatoes, or 2 tins of whole tomatoes

2 large onions, sliced

2 tbsp olive oil

1 or 2 small dry, chopped chillies (or a pinch of chilli powder)

1 tbsp sugar

3 garlic cloves, crushed

Chopped basil leaves

Black pepper

Cook sliced onion in olive oil over low heat until it becomes transparent.

Stir in the chopped chillies (or the chilli powder), crushed garlic, sugar, pepper, and chopped basil leaves.

Press peeled, fresh tomatoes, or tinned tomatoes through strainer.

Add to onion mixture and simmer slowly without covering until a smooth, thick consistency is achieved.

Allow to cool before using or storing in glass jars.

Note: This sauce keeps well in the refrigerator.

HARISSA

Harissa is a fiery-hot chilli pureé that is used to season North African dishes. It is used in couscous, and meat dishes. While it can be bought from continental food stores, it is best made fresh.

Makes 1/3 of a cup

30 g dried hot red chillies

1 tspn caraway seeds

1/2 tspn cumin seed

1/2 tspn coriander seed

2 garlic cloves, peeled

1 tbsp water

4 tbsp olive oil

When handling chillies it is advisable to wear rubber gloves.

Put the dried chillies in a bowl and pour on enough hot water to cover. Let them soak for at least an hour.

Meanwhile, grind the spices together in a spice mill or with a pestle and mortar.

Drain the chillies, then pat them dry with paper towels, and chop. Grind them together with the garlic and spices.

Add the water and 3 tbsp of olive oil, mix well and transfer to a jar. Spoon the remaining oil over the top, cover tightly, and refrigerate.

It will keep for months and is only used a teaspoon at a time for flavouring.

MY OWN 'NAISE
(Mayonnaise)

Making your own mayonnaise is simple and rewarding culinary magic which transforms several liquid ingredients into a delicious thick cream.

Make in a blender in moments or the traditional way in a bowl with a fork or egg whisk. It will keep for several days in an airtight container in the refrigerator and you can call it YOUR OWN 'NAISE!

Ingredients

1 egg yolk
1 cup olive oil (I use light olive oil)
2 tbsp good wine vinegar or juice of one lemon (or a mixture of both!)
1 tspn Dijon mustard
Pepper to season

Put the egg yolk, lemon juice and/or vinegar and mustard into the bowl and mix or blend well.

Slowly add the oil, drop by drop.

As the mixture thickens, you can increase the rate at which you add the oil.

When all the oil is added the mixture will resemble a thick, creamy sauce. Season to taste.

Tip: I use balsamic vinegar in this recipe. It is good quality and has matured like good wine over several months. Your mayonnaise will be smoother and less acidic than if made with other vinegars. If you cannot get balsamic vinegar, use good wine vinegar.

Tip: If the mixture curdles as a result of adding the oil too quickly, it is simple to repair the emulsion by putting another egg yolk into a new bowl and very slowly dribbling the curdled mixture into the egg yolk as slowly as you should have previously added the oil.

GRAPEFRUIT DRESSING

Makes a cup of dressing

2 ruby grapefruit
(or other variety but ruby are best)
2 tspn horseradish sauce
Good sized sprig fresh rosemary
1/2 cup virgin olive oil
2 tbsp honey (I use red gum or
leatherwood)
Freshly ground black pepper

The grapefruit is one of our newer fruits.

It has only been around for a couple of hundred years, originating in the West Indies and it is a cross between the orange and the pommelo, another large citrus fruit.

My favourite variety is the ruby grapefruit, with its pink flesh, which was discovered in Texas in the late twenties.

One of the few places in the world where ruby grapefruit grows is Carnarvon in Western Australia, about 900 kilometres north of Perth.

It is no wonder it is in great demand. It has a beautiful sweet flavour as it is or grilled for 4 or 5 minutes.

It doesn't need added sugar. It's also great in salads and salad dressings.

I have borrowed this recipe from another grapefruit lover, Brian Ferguson, Corporate Executive Chef of Australian Airlines .

Cut the top and bottom off one of the grapefruit and peel by cutting down right through to the flesh, cutting away the rind, pith and skin, following the line of the fruit.

Then cut out the individual segments by cutting next to the membrane of each segment.

In a bowl, mix the juice of the other grapefruit, the olive oil, honey, about a tablespoon of finely chopped rosemary (if you are using dried rosemary, use only half a teaspoon), the horseradish sauce and black pepper. Mix well.

Finally stir in the grapefruit segments.

This beautiful, fruity salad dressing works particularly well with smoked fish.

YOGHURT MINT DRESSING

Yoghurt is simply fermented milk. It is a food which has been with us for centuries and is said to be associated with both good health and longevity. Although Australians usually eat yoghurt made from cows milk, in Turkey, goat and sheep yoghurt is eaten, while in Egypt, water buffalo milk is used for yoghurt.

Serves 4

1 cup natural low fat yoghurt
2 tbsp fresh chopped mint
1 tbsp honey
1 tspn lemon juice

Combine all ingredients and chill thoroughly before serving as a salad dressing, a sauce with cold seafood, a dip with vegetables, or as a refreshing side dish with hot curries.

SPICY PAWPAW SOUP

A beautiful spicy soup which may be served hot or cold; winter or summer.

Serves 6

1 large pawpaw
3 tbsp coconut milk
1 Spanish onion, finely chopped
2 cloves garlic, crushed and finely chopped
1 tspn grated ginger
1 tin chicken consommé
2 tspn chilli sauce
1 tbsp olive oil
1/2 tspn sesame oil
1 tspn ground coriander
1 tbsp chopped fresh coriander
2 limes

Gently cook onion, ginger and garlic in oils until onion is soft.

Scoop out pawpaw flesh (seeds removed) and add to onion mixture. Cook for 15 minutes. Add chicken consommé, coriander, chilli sauce, juice of 1 lime, coconut milk and continue cooking 5 minutes stirring constantly. Do not allow to boil once coconut milk has been added.

Stir in juice of second lime just before serving.

Season to taste and serve garnished with sprinkling of fresh coriander.

Fish and Seafood

 Fish continue to frighten people. I don't mean sharks and piranhas, but the every day fish that stares up at you from the fishmonger's slab. I am sure that part of the fear comes from the challenge presented in preparing fish for cooking, yet it is as easy to deal with as meat. And it is in plentiful supply in Australia. Although it is rarely as cheap as meat, it may be enjoyed in smaller quantities and it is certainly more economical to buy whole fish than fillets.

Nutritionists recommend we eat fish at least three times a week because it is a good balance of protein and fat. A few fishy tips:

Buying. Look the fish in the eye. It should be bright and bulging out, not sunken. The flesh should be firm and smell fresh and saline (if it is a sea fish). There should be no smell of ammonia. The scales should be firmly attached and the gills should be red.

Frozen fish. Today it is possible to buy fish caught yesterday several thousand kilometres away. It is snap frozen on the boat as soon as it is caught. However, it is unwise to freeze fish in a conventional domestic freezer since it freezes slowly causing ice crystals to form in the flesh. This damages its texture. Always allow fish to thaw slowly. Dry thoroughly before cooking.

To scale a fish. Remove the fins with a small sharp knife. Holding the tail, scrape the scales away from you down towards the head. Make sure all scales are removed then wash and dry the fish. If the fish is slimy pour boiling water over it, drain and then it will be easier to scale.

Cleaning. You will normally buy the fish without entrails. Nevertheless it is a good idea to wash the interior of the fish with salted water and dry with kitchen towel.

POACHED OCEAN TROUT

Serves 2 to 6, depending on the size of the trout

1 ocean trout
1 cup fish or chicken stock
1/2 bottle of fruity white wine
Juice of 1 lemon and the squeezed halves

1 medium onion finely sliced
1 cup chopped fresh parsley
1 tspn freshly ground black pepper
1 bay leaf
4 or 5 cloves

When you think of farming, the sea probably doesn't immediately spring to mind.

Yet it is in the crystal clear waters surrounding Tasmania that one of the world's best taste sensations is being farmed: the Salmonidae family of Atlantic salmon and ocean trout.

Ocean farming is still in its infancy in Australia but it promises to have a huge impact on the way we eat in the future as it appears that the ocean trout, native of Northern Europe, actually grows better down under.

Ocean trout has a succulent pink flesh and a delightful delicate flavour. Although it may be grilled, baked or barbecued, I find it is perfect poached in white wine.

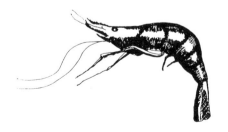

Wash fish in cold water and place in a fish kettle or baking pan. (I leave the head on because it adds flavour to the poaching liquor)

Add all the other ingredients and enough water to just cover fish.

Put lid on kettle or cover pan with foil and simmer very gently. If in a kettle, simmer on top of stove over very low heat. If in a baking pan, cook in oven that is no hotter than 150°C.

An average size ocean trout will take about 20 minutes to cook.

When you think it is cooked, test it by putting a knife in the flesh - if it flakes it

Poached Ocean Trout (recipe page 80)

Crayfish Taylor (recipe page 81)

Honey King Prawns (recipe page 85)

Fresh Tuna Salad (recipe page 91)

is cooked. Another test is to look at its eyes - if they are white the fish is cooked. Remove the fish and drain. You can reduce the liquor and use it as a sauce.

Serve hot or cold with mild flavoured vegetables, plain boiled potatoes, a big green salad and why not a glass of the wine you used in the cooking liquor to complement the meal.

Fact: Apart from adding flavour, the citric acid in lemons will help keep fish flesh firm.

EXPLODING A MYTH

It is a culinary myth that poor wine may be used in cooking. If a wine is not worth drinking it is not worth cooking with. Throw it away. Life's too short to drink bad wine!

CRAYFISH TAYLOR

One of Western Australia's most successful industries is the catching and marketing of rock lobsters, or as the West Aussies call them, crays.

More than a billion dollars has been invested in the industry and that investment pumps about 250 million dollars back into the economy each year.

While Australians themselves are big consumers of this delicacy, 98% of the rock lobster is exported, mostly to Asia.

The opening of the season is celebrated in Fremantle with a frenzy of feasting on a meal prepared from the first catch. (You could say the patrons go crayzee!)

One of the most effective recipes using crayfish belongs to Chris Taylor, Executive Chef of Western Australia's Observation City Resort Hotel.

It preserves the subtle flavour of the seafood while adding gentle new flavours.

Serves 2 or 4 hungry lobster lovers

2 crayfish
1 lemongrass blade
1/2 red chilli or 1 tspn chilli sauce
1/2 cup chopped fresh parsley
50 ml wine vinegar
5 g white peppercorns
1 lime
1 tbsp chives

Combine parsley, peppercorns, half the vinegar and half the lemongrass (finely chopped) in water. Bring to boil.

Split crayfish lengthwise. Discard grit from the head. Lift flesh from the shell and replace. This will enable flesh to be taken out of the shell more easily when cooked.

Put crays into a steamer. Spoon over remainder of lemongrass (sliced), thinly sliced chilli (seeds excluded) or 1 tspn chilli sauce and place over boiling liquid. Cover and steam for about 12 minutes until almost cooked. Remove from heat.

Reduce small ladle of steaming liquid and the remaining wine vinegar by two thirds. Finish by stirring in juice of the lime.

Strain into warmed sauce boat and add chopped chives.

To serve, place pre-heated plates on table with steam basket in the middle accompanied by milled pepper and a green salad with a lemon and olive oil dressing. Steamed or boiled potatoes are a good accompaniment.

It is a good idea to buy lobsters live and immerse them in fresh water before cooking Cook in boiling water with 1/2 lemon and 1 tbsp sugar for 10 - 12 minutes.

FISH WITH PAWPAW SAUCE

An easy recipe suitable for any white fish fillets. I prefer the delicately flavoured pink snapper caught in the Indian Ocean at Shark Bay in Western Australia.

Serves 4

500g fish fillets
250g fresh pawpaw flesh
1 tspn ground coriander
1/2 cup coconut milk
1/2 tspn sesame oil
1 tspn grated ginger root
1 lemongrass root or a couple of lemongrass blades (optional)
6 spring onions
2 limes (or 1 lemon)
2 tbsp olive oil
1 cup chicken or fish stock

Chop the white part of the spring onion and cook gently in a frying pan with the grated ginger in 1 tbsp of olive oil for a couple of minutes.

While that is cooking, remove the flesh from the pawpaw and mash with a fork. Add this to the pan and cook until it is thoroughly softened.

Stir in the chicken (or fish) stock, the coconut milk, sesame oil, and the ground coriander. Toss in the lemongrass and leave to simmer gently while you attend to the fish.

Make sure the fillets are dry by wiping with kitchen towel then fry them gently with the rest of the oil. Cook for 2 or 3 minutes on each side. Don't overcook. Transfer to warm plate and keep warm in a low oven.

By now the sauce should be cooked. Squeeze in the juice of 1 lime or 1/2 lemon. Strain the sauce. Pour any juices from the fish fillets into the sauce. Stir then pour over fish.

Garnish with slices of fresh lime or lemon and fresh coriander or Vietnamese mint (similar to coriander) and plain rice.

Tip: Fish should only be turned once during cooking. I start with the skin side up, cook it, then turn it. This way, it is easier to see if it is cooked. The flesh should be flaky.

TRIED

IN-A-HURRY CURRY

A simple and quick-to-prepare mild, fish curry. It cooks in about 40 minutes.

Serves 4 to 6

1 kg white fish fillets, cubed (I prefer trevally or snapper)

3 large cloves of garlic, finely chopped

1 large onion

1 tspn chilli sauce

2 tbsp olive oil

5 cardamon pods

300 ml chicken or fish stock

1/4 cup coconut milk (available in supermarkets)

1 tspn fresh ginger, finely chopped

1 tspn cumin powder

1 tspn ground coriander

Garnish: fresh coriander or parsley

Black pepper to season

Fry onion with garlic and ginger in olive oil until onion has softened.

Stir in cardamon pods, chilli sauce, cumin, ground coriander. Cook 2 or 3 minutes.

Warm chicken stock, stir in coconut milk.

Fold fish pieces into herb and spice mixture. Add stock/coconut milk mixture.

Cover and simmer over very low heat for 30 minutes or until fish is cooked.

Do not stir during the cooking.

Garnish with chopped, fresh coriander or parsley and season with pepper.

SALMON TARTARE

Really fresh fish need not be cooked at all. In this recipe fresh salmon is slightly pickled in lemon juice.

I use fresh Atlantic salmon, but ocean trout can also be used.

Serves 4

1 ripe avocado
Juice of 1 lemon
200 g fresh salmon, thinly sliced
A few leaves of fresh basil
2 or 3 oven, or sun-dried tomatoes
2 tbsp ricotta
A few cherry tomatoes to garnish
Mixed lettuce

Mash the avocado flesh with half the lemon juice. This will prevent the avocado from discolouring.

Place in the centre of a dinner plate and pile on a quantity of mixed lettuces.

Add thinly sliced salmon. Squeeze remaining lemon juice over the fish.

Decorate with the remaining ingredients with a topping of ricotta and a few thinly sliced dried tomatoes and fresh cherry tomatoes. A delicious lunch-time dish.

HONEY KING PRAWNS

A spicy recipe, very quickly prepared, that was borrowed from the Chinese.

Serves 4

*500g fresh, raw, peeled prawns
(preferably large ones)*

1/2 cup honey

1 tbsp reduced salt soy sauce

1/2 cup sherry

1 tspn sesame oil

Pepper

1/2 tspn five spice

1 piece of ginger, peeled and chopped

2 or 3 small hot chillies, chopped

3 cloves of garlic, chopped

2 tbsp sesame seeds

3 spring onions, chopped

1 tbsp olive oil

Make sauce by mixing honey, soy sauce, sherry, sesame oil, pepper, and five spice.

Cook ginger, chillies, and garlic gently in oil for about 2 minutes. Do not let them brown. Remove from the pan.

Increase heat, cook the prawns a few at a time for about 1 minute. They should not be thoroughly cooked. Remove and put in a warm place. Repeat till all prawns have been pre-cooked.

Put ginger, chillies and garlic back in the pan, add sauce, reduce to a syrupy consistency.

Toss prawns in sauce until coated and prawns are cooked thoroughly.

Remove from heat, sprinkle with sesame seeds, toss. Serve topped with chopped spring onions.

Tip: Prawns do not need very much cooking. A good, fresh prawn can be eaten raw. Ask the Japanese! It is better to have them slightly undercooked than overcooked.

SCAMPI A LA CAMANDOULE

A wonderful recipe from the Moulin de la Camandoule in Southern France.

Although the chef used scampi, king prawns could be substituted. I have also deleted his cream to make a lighter sauce.

Serves 6

24 medium-sized scampi
1 green cabbage
1 orange
1 tbsp of orange peel, finely chopped
4 sprigs of coriander
1/2 tspn curry powder
1/2 tspn ground ginger
1/2 tspn cardamon powder
1 tbsp white breadcrumbs
200 ml fish or chicken stock
Freshly milled black pepper

Cut the cabbage in quarters, chop finely in the direction of its width.

Blanch quickly in boiling water, rinse in cold water, drain, and leave on a plate.

Make a mixture of orange peel, breadcrumbs and the powdered spices.

Peel the scampi and keep the carcasses for the sauce.

Roll each tail in the mixed spices and breadcrumbs. Place on greaseproof paper and put aside.

Prepare the sauce by simmering the scampi carcasses for 25 minutes in the stock over a low heat. Pass the stock through a fine sieve. Reduce to a thick consistency.

Just before serving, quickly fry the scampi tails and reheat the cabbage by tossing in pan with a pinch of orange peel.

Make 4 little piles of cabbage on each plate, pour the sauce over the cabbage, dress with 4 scampi tails per plate.

At the last moment, add a few sprigs of coriander and sprinkle with black pepper from a pepper mill.

STUFFED BABY SQUID

Also from France, this is a speciality of Chez Antoine in the French city of Aix-en-Provence, the capital of Provençale cuisine.

A delightful combination of subtle flavours that can be served any time.

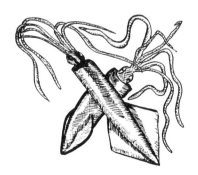

Serves 6

12 small squid
200 g of cooked rice
15 g ham, finely chopped
50 g reduced fat mozzarella,
finely chopped
1 large onion, finely chopped
500 ml tomato sauce (best if you use
homemade - see page 74)
6 garlic cloves
1/2 tspn saffron
(This will add colour and a subtle
saffron flavour to the dish)
Freshly ground black pepper
1 tbsp olive oil
1 tbsp brandy (optional)
1 tbsp chopped parsley

Clean the squid, keeping tubes and bits. Chop the bits finely and cook them for two or three minutes with the chopped onion. Pour off residual water.

Add chopped ham, rice, cheese, saffron, two of the crushed garlic cloves, half the onion and 1/2 tspn of brandy.

Fill the squid tubes with this mixture and hold shut with tooth picks.

Put them in a pan with the remainder of the onion, brandy, and oil. Cover with the tomato sauce and cook over a very low heat for about 15-20 minutes, depending on the size of the squid.

Serve with plain rice and a freshly tossed salad of mixed lettuces.

DAM FINE YABBIES

In most dams on farms in Southern Australia live thousands of happy, little freshwater crayfish, also known as yabbies or marron. Up until now their only worry was the farmer fishing them out of the dam for his dinner.

But now things are changing. There is a world-wide marketing campaign to promote this fresh-water crustacean, and so far they have been accepted internationally as a quality, gourmet seafood.

Serves 4 to 6

750 g yabbies
125 ml lime or lemon juice
Fresh, black pepper
2 stalks of celery
1 ripe honeydew melon
100 g snow peas
2 tspn coriander

Remove shell from yabbies and place the meat in lime juice. Marinate for 2 hours.

Cut celery into julienne strips. Scoop melon out with a melon baller. Top the snowpeas, blanch quickly in boiling water and refresh in cold water. Combine celery, honeydew, peas and coriander.

Drain the yabbies and toss with the other ingredients.

DRESSING

5 ml ginger juice.
(Place a small piece of ginger in a garlic crusher and squeeze.)
10 ml lemon juice
40 ml olive oil
Pepper to taste

Mix thoroughly. Drizzle over salad.

MARINATED PRAWNS WITH FENNEL

Fennel is a natural partner for seafood. Its slightly aniseed flavour complements it beautifully.

Don't be frightened by all the olive oil in this recipe as it is all drained away before you eat these mouth watering prawns.

Serves 4 to 6

1.5 kg green prawns
1 bulb of fennel roughly chopped
3 lemons sliced paper thin
2 cups olive oil

MARINADE

1 tspn chilli powder or sauce
1 tspn fennel seeds
6 cloves garlic peeled and sliced
2 bay leaves crushed

Mix together chilli powder, fennel seeds, garlic and crushed bay leaves.

Shell and clean prawns, cook in boiling water for 2 minutes - no longer or they will be spoiled. They will float to the surface when cooked.

Layer warm prawns, fennel and lemon slices in a bowl, season each layer with chilli mix.

Pour over oil and refrigerate for at least 12 hours.

Drain well and garnish with fresh bay leaves and serve with crusty bread.

SMOKED TROUT SALAD

Smoking is an old but excellent way of preserving food while enhancing its flavour.

The natural oils in trout make it one of the best foods to undergo the smoking process leaving the flesh soft and tender and the taste subtle.

Serves 4

2 smoked trout
100 g mixed lettuce (radiccio, butter, iceberg, and baby spinach)
1 burpless cucumber
1 Spanish onion, finely sliced
1 tbsp balsamic vinegar
1 tbsp extra virgin olive oil

Peel and bone trout. Flake into a bowl.

Peel cucumber and cut into thin strips. Place lettuce mixture in the centre of a large serving plate.

Place onions and cucumber on top of lettuce, and the trout on top of all of this.

Drizzle balsamic vinegar and oil over the salad and serve.

GRILLED SARDINES WITH LEMON

One of the big names in the fishing industry is *Sardinops neopilchardus*. It is a big name for a very small fish: the sardine.

In the past we have thought of sardines as those oily little things packed shoulder to shoulder in tiny flat tins with a key to open them which either got lost or just didn't work.

The sardines that were caught in Australia were usually sold frozen in blocks as bait.

Now the tide has turned and fresh sardines have become a popular gourmet food rich in healthy fish oils.

Serves 4

12-16 fresh sardines (about 750 g)
1 tbsp olive oil
2 cloves garlic, finely chopped
Juice of 2 lemons and 1 tspn grated lemon rind
12 fresh basil leaves, finely chopped
Freshly ground pepper

Clean the sardines by cutting a small incision along the belly and scooping out the insides with your finger.

Rinse the fish thoroughly under cold water and drain. Pat dry with paper towels and lay on a plate.

Sprinkle the fish with pepper and toss with olive oil.

Let sit for 15 minutes, turning once.

Preheat the grill. Place the sardines on the grill or rack.

Grill for 2 minutes. Turn and continue to grill for 2 more minutes, they should flake easily when done.

Remove the sardines from the heat, allow to cool.

When they are cool enough to handle remove the skins.

Lay the fish on a serving dish and add a little more pepper.

Sprinkle with garlic and lemon juice. Let marinate for 1 hour.

Just before serving, sprinkle with remaining lemon juice, lemon rind and basil.

Divide the sardines equally among plates and serve with salad.

I suggest fairly hearty salads such as Potato Maroc (See page 52), and Capsicum Caper (See page 42) as accompaniments.

SARDINE ESCABECHE

Escabeche is a Spanish method for pickling fish.

It's a great way of using up surplus fish.

This recipe is ideal for barbecues but the fish could also be grilled.

Serves 4

2 kgs sardines or other smaller fish

1 tbsp olive oil

2 garlic cloves

Pinch saffron threads, or just a touch of
saffron powder

Pinch ground ginger

Freshly ground black pepper

4 tbsp red wine vinegar

3 tbsp water

1 shallot or spring onion, minced

1 lemon, sliced

2 small bay leaves

Clean, wash and dry fish, toss with olive oil and pepper. Barbecue or grill for about 2 1/2 minutes each side. Do not overcook. Transfer to baking dish or casserole.

Pound the garlic in a mortar along with the saffron and ginger. Mix in the vinegar, water and shallot.

Toss with the fish. Add the lemon slices and bay leaves, cover and refrigerate overnight. Before you serve it you may need to add more pepper.

This dish will keep for a few days in the fridge. I serve it with fresh salads and focaccia.

FRESH TUNA SALAD

A delightful salad of tuna that is pickled in a mixture of soy sauce and rice wine.

Serves 4

250 g of fresh tuna, thinly sliced
against the grain

1 tbsp reduced salt soy sauce

1 tbsp rice wine or sherry

1/2 Spanish onion, chopped

2 tbsp wine vinegar

1 tbsp fresh coriander, chopped

1 tbsp olive oil

1 tspn sesame oil

1 avocado, peeled and sliced

2 cups of plain steamed rice

Combine the soy and rice wine, add the tuna and marinate for 20 minutes.

Mix together the onion, vinegar, coriander and oils.

Place rice in centre of large plate. Arrange the avocado and spoon the sauce over the top. Finally remove the tuna from the marinade and pile on top of the avocado.

Garnish with a sprig of coriander.

FISH'N FOR COMPLIMENTS

Whole fish baked with spices and coconut milk. Serve this and you'll be praised right through the meal.

Serves 4

1 whole fish (about 1.5 kg), scaled
3 tspn turmeric
2 cloves garlic, finely chopped
2 tspn finely chopped ginger
2 tbsp chopped coriander or Vietnamese mint
Juice and grated rind of 1 lemon
2 tspn ground coriander
2 tspn sesame oil
1 tbsp coconut cream
Freshly ground black pepper
A few breadcrumbs
Garnish: spring onions, chopped

Wash and dry fish with paper towels, inside and out. Rub inside and out with turmeric.

Mix other ingredients adding breadcrumbs until a paste is formed. Place inside fish.

Wrap in foil and bake in oven at 180°C until just cooked (about 35 minutes). If the eyes are white and the fish flakes it will be done, beautifully. Serve on a bed of rice, garnished with spring onions.

MARINATIONS

Rich oily fish are perfect for grilling or barbecueing since they remain moist. This marinade makes an excellent complement to any strongly flavoured dish.

Serves 6

1 kg fish fillets or steaks (mackerel or sardines)
1 glass dry sherry
1 tspn chilli sauce
2 tbsp low salt soy sauce
1/2 tspn sesame oil
1 tbsp honey
Juice of 1 lime
3 of 4 spring onions, finely chooped

Boil all ingredients (except spring onions) in a saucepan and reduce by a third. Allow to cool then add spring onions.

Place fish in a dish and marinate for 2 hours at room temperature. Drain and barbecue fish, basting frequently.

Poultry

These days when we talk of poultry we usually mean chicken - unless we are talking turkey, which is still a once-a-year treat for most of us.

The chicken was first domesticated in India, where its ancestor was the wild red jungle fowl, *Gallus gallus* .

Apparently, these birds were shy and easily angered and were regarded as sacred. They appeared in religious ceremonies at which their entrails were examined in search of the meaning of life. It's no wonder they were easily angered.

Recipes using chicken were first published as far back as Roman times in the writings of Apicius, one of the earliest foodies. Since then chicken has become the world's most popular source of meat.

In Australia alone annual commercial production exceeds 300 million birds. Compare that with only 3 million in 1950.

A somewhat paltry figure!

The reasons for its popularity are price and versatility. Chicken is inexpensive and there are very few meat dishes that cannot be made with its meat. It is also a great source of protein, iron, zinc and riboflavin.

Most of the fat is in the skin so it's a good idea to remove it before cooking.

I prefer fresh birds to the frozen variety. When selecting a chicken, the meat should be firm and the point of the breastbone should be soft and flexible.

Remove plastic wrapping as soon as you get the bird home.

Wipe dry with paper towel and store loosely covered in the refrigerator.

Since poultry is susceptible to bacteria, make sure it is handled with washed hands, use clean equipment and wash it and your hands after handling.

You should make it a rule never to handle raw and cooked chicken at the same time.

Before cooking the chicken should be allowed to warm to room temperature - that includes frozen birds, which should be thoroughly thawed.

If stuffing the chicken, it is a good idea always to do it just before cooking, especially if the stuffing is warm when placed inside the bird.

Allow extra cooking time for a stuffed chicken. And make sure you allow a considerable amount of time if you are cooking a whole stuffed emu!

I have included emu with these recipes. (Apologies to the wild red jungle fowl!)

CHICKEN DIJONNAIS

TRIED AFFXS

This dish is one of my favourite food temptations.

It is simple to prepare with a distinctive flavour all its own.

Serves 4

500 g skinned chicken pieces
(preferably on the bone - leg pieces are ideal)

1 glass white wine
1 cup chicken stock
2 tbsp brandy (optional)
2 tbsp olive oil
2 cloves garlic
1 dspn smooth Dijon mustard
Few sprigs of fresh thyme (or tarragon)
Freshly ground pepper

Pat chicken pieces dry with kitchen paper and brown in frying pan with the olive oil.

Flambé with the brandy.

Add wine, peeled and crushed garlic, Dijon mustard, pepper, chicken stock and thyme. Mix well.

Cover and leave to simmer over very low heat for 40 minutes.

Remove the thyme and serve.

Good accompaniments for this splendid dish are plain boiled or microwaved potatoes and broccoli, which is a member of the brassica family and is related to mustard. Big family, the brassicas.

Despite having quite a lot of Dijon mustard in it, this dish will not finish up with an overpowering mustard flavour.

And you won't need to add salt.

Tip: When flambéeing, it is a good idea to warm the alcohol before pouring it into the pan. Then have a lighted match in one hand and the brandy in a container in the other. Pour the brandy over the meat and touch the flame to the vapour.

WARNING

This procedure is not recommended in kitchens with low ceilings.

CHICKEN TOMATO TREAT

One of the most delightful taste combinations is tomatoes with chicken.

The Italians acknowledge the fact with their pollo al cacciatora, as do the French with poulet à la provençale. Here is an Australian recipe which brings together the best of the French and Italian dishes - a combination of chicken pieces cooked with olive oil, tomatoes, garlic and sherry. I like to start with a whole chicken so I can use the carcass to make a chicken stock for the dish.

Serves 4

---

*1 roasting chicken, jointed into pieces
with skin removed*

2 tbsp virgin olive oil

500 g fresh or tinned tomatoes

1 glass dry sherry

1 clove of garlic

Handful of fresh basil

Brown chicken pieces in a little olive oil along with cloves of garlic in their skins. (If you are a garlic wimp you can remove cloves later.) I use virgin oil because this dish benefits from the flavour of olives.

Over high heat, flambé with a glass of dry sherry.

Do not worry about the alcohol which will evaporate leaving the beautiful sherry flavours.Once the flame has gone out, add tomatoes.

Cover and simmer very, very slowly for about 40 minutes. (You should hear a gentle 'bloopbloop' rather than a noisy 'hubblabubblabbla'.)

Once cooked, remove the chicken pieces to a warm dish and keep warm.

Remove the garlic and discard unless you like garlic as much as I do. In which case, squeeze the softened garlic from the skin and put into the sauce, discarding the skins.

Reduce the sauce to a thick consistency and pour over the chicken pieces.

Add chopped fresh basil leaves and serve. (I do not recommend dried basil, even small amounts are likely to overpower the dish.)

A perfect accompaniment for this richly flavoured dish is plain noodles tossed in

some finely chopped parsley, garlic and lemon rind - a combination of flavours the Italians call gremolata, and which traditionally accompanies their famous veal dish, Osso Bucco. (See page 119)

It goes equally well with chicken.

> *A word about roasting a whole chicken in the oven. Although it's commonly roasted breast up, it makes much more sense to roast it the other way up, on the breast. That way, gravity will draw the juices from the back into the breast keeping the breast meat moist.*

CHICKEN COUSCOUS ✓ FRE L.

Couscous is a traditional North African dish. It is served in rich and poor homes alike as the centre-piece to the evening meal.

Based on semolina it makes a good alternative to rice. It is usually accompanied by tagines (stews).

This dish combines couscous with a chicken tagine.

Lemon Chicken (recipe page 98)

Previous pages, Chicken Dijonnais (recipe page 94)   *Siamese Chicken (recipe page 101)*

Serves 6 to 8

CHICKEN TAGINE

*1 chicken, skin removed and trimmed of
all fat, cut into 8 pieces*

1 tbsp olive oil

2 large onions, sliced

4 to 6 garlic cloves, minced

2 carrots, sliced

2 turnips, peeled and sliced

2 celery stalks, sliced

1 tspn ground cumin

1/2 tspn ground ginger

1/2 tspn ground turmeric

1 bay leaf

1 cup dry white wine

2 1/2 cups chicken stock

1 tspn paprika

1 cup cooked chick-peas

*1/8 tspn powdered saffron or pinch of
saffron threads*

2 small zucchini, sliced

3 to 4 tbsp fresh lemon juice

Cayenne pepper

1/4 cup chopped fresh coriander

2 tbsp chopped fresh parsley

Heat the olive oil in a large flameproof
casserole over medium heat.

Fry the onions and garlic, stirring until

the onions are tender. This should take
between 5 and 10 minutes. Add the carrots,
turnips and celery and cook a further
couple of minutes.

Add the chicken, cumin, ginger, turmeric,
bay leaf, white wine and chicken stock,
stir together and bring to a simmer.

Simmer for 45-60 minutes stirring
occasionally until chicken is very tender
and falling off the bone. Add the paprika,
chick-peas, saffron, zucchini, and lemon
juice, simmer a further 15 minutes.

Check flavour and add cayenne to taste.
Stir in coriander and parsley just before
serving.

COUSCOUS

350 g semolina

2 cups chicken or vegetable stock

1 tspn harissa (see page 75)

*Garnish: coriander leaves and lemon
slices*

Lightly oil an ovenproof serving dish.
Place the semolina and harissa in the dish
and pour the stock over it.

Place in a moderate oven (180°C) for 10
minutes. It should have absorbed the liquid

and have a thick consistency.

Stir the semolina with a kitchen fork.

If you do not plan to serve it straight away, cover and keep it warm in a low oven.

When you are ready to serve, bring the chicken tagine to a simmer and fluff the semolina one more time with a fork.

Spoon onto plates, then ladle the chicken and vegetables and some of the broth over the semolina.

Garnish each plate with coriander leaves and lemon slices.

LEMON CHICKEN

The lemon is a wonderful fruit and we should make more use of it in cooking, for both its juice and its rind. This recipe combines chicken and lemon in a simply prepared dish with a taste of the orient.

I use thigh pieces - being on the bone, they don't dry out, so they are the best parts to have in a dish which is simmered.

Serves 4

1 kg lean skinless chicken pieces.
2 tspn finely chopped ginger
1 tbsp reduced salt soy sauce
1 glass dry sherry
1 tspn sesame oil
Juice and grated rind of 1 large or 2 small lemon(s)
2 tbsp honey
1 tspn olive oil
Spring onions (to garnish)
Lemon slices (to garnish)

Marinate the skinned chicken pieces in the soy sauce and the sesame oil for anything between an hour and a day.

Make up a sauce using the grated lemon rind, lemon juice, the honey and the sherry, mix well.

Drain the chicken, reserving the marinade. Pat the pieces dry with a kitchen towel and brown them in olive oil along with the ginger.

When browned, pour in lemon and honey mixture and marinade, cover and let simmer for about 40 minutes.

As always when simmering, just a very low heat, (bloopbloop sounds).

When the dish is cooked you'll find that the sauce is not a thick one, but that's perfectly alright. Gone are the days when we have to thicken all sauces with flour. But you can remove the chicken and reduce the sauce to make it thicker if you wish.

Garnish with chopped spring onions and some slices of lemon and serve with plain rice.

ORIENTAL CHICKEN KEBABS

Pieces of chicken breasts, marinated with sesame oil and soy sauce, and barbecued on skewers with tomatoes.

Serves 4

1/2 kg skinless chicken breasts
2 tspn sesame oil
4 tspn light soy sauce
1/2 kg small tomatoes cut into quarters and seeded

Cut chicken into bite-sized pieces and marinate for several hours or overnight in a mixture of sesame oil and soy sauce.

Thread chicken onto kebab or bamboo skewers, alternating with tomato pieces.

Brush with marinade and barbecue or grill for 2 or 3 minutes taking care not to overcook as meat will dry out.

As with all barbecues these are great served with lots of different flavoured salads.

Tip: Soak wooden skewers in water overnight to prevent them burning on the barbecue.

CHICKEN CASABLANCA

A colourful dish which could have been Humphrey Bogart's favourite when shooting the film Casablanca in Morocco!

Serves 6

1 roasting chicken about 1.5-1.75kg (skin removed and trimmed of all fat)

1/4 tspn each of paprika, powdered cumin and ground black pepper

4 tbsp extra virgin olive oil

350g black olives, thinly sliced

1/2 tspn saffron, powdered or strands

100 g chick peas, soaked overnight and drained

Chicken stock

3 onions, sliced

2 tbsp chopped parsley (flat-leafed if you can find it)

2 tbsp fresh green coriander

Lemon juice

Wipe chicken dry.

Cut into serving pieces and season as generously as you like with paprika and cumin. Add freshly ground pepper to taste. Leave for an hour or two for flavours to infuse.

In 1 tbsp of olive oil in a large frying pan or deep flame proof casserole, sauté chicken pieces with onions until golden.

Sprinkle with saffron.

Skin and add the chickpeas (their little skins should slide off if they have been soaked sufficiently).

Add olives and chicken stock to barely cover, and gently simmer for an hour, or until the chicken is tender.

Toss chicken pieces with half the coriander and parsley. Put back in the sauce.

Garnish with remaining coriander and parsley and sprinkle with a few drops of lemon juice. Serve with rice.

√ ✓. Hot

SIAMESE CHICKEN

A simple spicy chicken dish with a hint of old Siam.

Serves 4

500 g chicken meat, chopped.
(best when it is taken from the breast
or thigh)

3 small hot, red chillies
Leaves from a bunch of fresh basil
2 tbsp of fresh mint, chopped
3 tbsp coriander, chopped
2 tbsp fish sauce (which you can buy
from Asian supermarkets)
1 tspn sesame oil
1 tbsp olive oil

Heat a wok or large frying pan until it starts to smoke.

Add the oils then stir fry the chicken until it changes colour.

Add half the basil, all the mint, chillies, parsley and fish sauce, stirring constantly.

Serve with plain rice and sprinkle with remaining basil.

BARBECUED EMU MEDALLIONS

✓

One of the newcomers to our dinner tables is emu.

At last this low fat meat is appearing in restaurants and gourmet food stores.

Because of its leaness it's superb cooked quickly on a barbecue and served with a simple sauce. It can also be baked.

Serves 4

350 g emu medallions
1 glass red wine
1 onion, 1 carrot, and 1 leek, finely
chopped
1 stick celery, finely chopped
12 juniper berries
A few sprigs thyme
Juice and chopped rind of 1 orange

Mix ingredients together to make a marinade in a stainless steel, glass or ceramic bowl.

Add medallions of emu, stir well and refrigerate overnight.

The next day...

Drain meat, reserving marinade.

Barbecue meat until just cooked.

Reduce marinade till it becomes a thick sauce. Pour over emu pieces.

Serve with simply cooked baby root vegetables.

SPICY ROAST EMU WITH BALSAMIC SAUCE

An interesting way to enjoy this delicious Australian addition to the world's poultry preferring palates.

Serves 4

2 emu fillets

6 or 7 cardamom pods

1 tspn ground coriander

3 cloves garlic, crushed and chopped finely

2 tbsp wine vinegar (preferably balsamic)

1 tbsp cracked black pepper

1 tbsp olive oil

1 tspn sesame oil

Crush the spices with garlic in mortar. Rub mixture over fillets, coating thickly.

Refrigerate for at least an hour.

Heat oils in pan, add fillets and brown on all sides.

Bake in baking tray at 210°C for 10 minutes. The emu will be a bit rare. This is fine - it is the best way to eat it.

Remove to warm place and allow to stand for 15 minutes.

BALSAMIC SAUCE

2 apples, peeled and finely chopped

1 cup beef consommé or stock

1 cup port

1 tbsp red currant jelly or honey

2 tbsp balsamic vinegar

Put all ingredients in pan and cook till reduced to thickish sauce.

Pour over the spicy roast emu fillets and serve with boiled potatoes and a leafy green salad.

A light Australian pinot noir is perfect with emu.

Meats

Once upon a time, actually about two years ago, meat meant red flesh. While beef and lamb are regarded as red meat, pork is being marketed in Australia as "the other white meat". In response to the increasing health awareness of today's consumers, producers are responding with leaner cuts. Recipes are also being tailored in recognition of the need to reduce the fat intake of our daily diet.

When selecting meat it has always been my view that it pays to develop a rapport with a good butcher, preferably one who knows and cares about cooking as well as about the meat he or she is selling. You can leave it to her or him to select the best cut.

Fresh meat should have a clear pink or red colour without signs of grey or yellow. Look for cuts which carry the tick of approval from the National Heart Foundation.

Meat should be stored loose-wrapped in the coldest part of the refrigerator . Minced meat and offal should be cooked the day it is bought. Large cuts may be kept for three or four days. Frozen meat will usually keep for up to six months in the freezer.

The flavour of meat can be enhanced by marinating in a mixture of light oil and wine or lemon juice along with the herbs and spices of your choice. During the marinating process, juicc is released from the meat so the marinade may be incorporated in the cooking. Veal should only be marinated for a couple of hours at most while other meats may be marinated overnight.

When cooking leaner cuts of meat the challenge is not to overcook them. With today's high standards of production, all meats may be safely cooked on the rare side - even pork. Remember, if it's "well-done" it's over-done and that's not well done at all!

PORK AND PRUNE STIR FRY

Stir frying is the art of almost burning food by frying it over big heat with a little oil. It is a very effective way to cook vegetables, fish and meat.

This dish brings together two distinct flavours - pork, and a fruit which for some reason has long been the source of ridicule, the prune. I cannot think why - it is high in fibre, tastes superb and beautifully complements pork.

Serves 6 to 8

1 kg lean pork (any cut will do)
1 large onion
3 or 4 spring onions
1/2 red capsicum
2 cloves garlic
1 tspn fresh ginger, chopped
1 tbsp light soy sauce
1 tspn sesame oil
1 glass sherry
2 tspn chilli sauce
1 tspn ground coriander
1 tbsp olive oil
1 dozen pitted prunes
Pinch black pepper
Fresh coriander to garnish
Juice of 1 lime

Trim any remaining fat from the meat and cut it into thin slices across the grain of the meat. (Chilling the meat in the freezer for an hour or so beforehand will make it easier to slice thinly.)

Mix up a marinade by combining the sesame oil, chilli sauce, the sherry, ground coriander and soy sauce.

Marinate the pork pieces in this aromatic mixture for a couple of hours or overnight.

Thinly slice the onion, coarsely slice the spring onions (white and green parts), and crush the garlic. Cut the pitted prunes and capsicum longways into strips.

Drain the pork pieces reserving the marinade.

In a wok or frying pan over high heat, fry onion, capsicum strips and garlic in some of the olive oil until onions begin to brown. A couple of minutes will do.

Remove to a dish or plate.

Put a dribble more oil into wok or pan. Add the pork pieces and stir.

The pan must be very hot otherwise the meat will toughen.

After a couple of minutes, toss in prunes to warm them. Sprinkle in chopped spring onions.

I add a little ground black pepper at this time along with the onions, capsicum and garlic. Toss a little more and serve with plain rice and a mixed green salad garnished with fresh or ground coriander and sprinkled with lime juice.

Delicious!

Tip: A wok or iron frying pan shouldn't be washed in soapy water. Just plain hot water will do. Smear it with oil before putting it away. That will stop it from rusting and will keep a good non-stick surface on the pan. When you're cooking a dish like this you need use less oil. And that makes good sense.

PORK AND ORANGE ROLL

Butcher Graham Jenkins of the Queen Victoria Market gave me this recipe.

It is a speciality from his own kitchen.

It is stuffed and roasted new-fashioned pork.

Serves 4 to 6

---

1 loin of pork (have your butcher trim off the fat and bone it)

2 tspn mixed dried herbs

Grated rind of 1 orange

1 tspn balsamic vinegar

1 onion, finely chopped

2 cloves garlic, crushed

Pinch of pepper

Breadcrumbs

With a very sharp, pointed knife, cut a pocket in the pork.

Mix herbs, orange rind, vinegar, onion, pepper and garlic. Add breadcrumbs until it just holds a ball shape if you scoop it up in your hands. Stuff into the pocket.

Close each end of pork with a satay stick. Bake at 160°C for about 25 minutes per kilogram. Test by inserting a satay stick or sharp knife in the meat. Juices should be clear.

Serve with boiled potatoes and steamed green vegetables.

PORK KEBABS

The marinade for these simple kebabs is one of the world's best and will ensure the meat stays moist and tender.

There's a hint of the Orient here as well.

It's been given the young persons' tick of approval. Children love it.

Serves 4

1/2 kg lean pork

2 apples

12 dried apricots

1 large onion

1 glass sherry

2 tbsp honey

2 tspn light soy sauce

1 tspn grated ginger

A few drops of sesame oil

1 cup good old Aussie salt reduced tomato sauce (the bottled kind)

Juice of 1/2 lemon

Chilli sauce or fresh or dried chillies (adults only)

Make a marinade by mixing sherry with honey, lemon juice, soy and tomato sauces, sesame oil, ginger and chilli.

Cut the pork into bite sized cubes and marinate for at least two hours. Leaving overnight will improve the effect. (What happens is that flavours infuse into the meat while the acid in the lemon juice works at tenderising it.)

Once marinated, drain pork pieces reserving the marinade.

Quarter the onion from top to bottom and break segments apart. Slice apples.

Thread pork pieces onto wooden kebab sticks alternating with onion quarters, apricots and apples, beginning and finishing with onion.

Cook on barbecue or under a grill, basting periodically with the marinade. Take care not to overcook. Like lamb or beef, it may be eaten on the rare side. Serve on plain rice with a side salad.

> *Reminder: Because there's acid from the lemon juice and tomato sauce, it's a good idea to use stainless steel, glass, ceramic or plastic bowl for marinating.*
>
> *Certainly not aluminium, which will react with the acid.*

GESTOOFD VARKENSSTUK (Pork Flemish Style)

It sounds insulting does it not?

In fact the Belgians, sandwiched as they are between France and Holland, have some of the finest dishes in the world, which they've managed to keep secret for centuries.

This dish combines lean pork with breadcrumbs, beer, and an unusual ingredient which gives a distinctive flavour: caraway.

Serves 8

1 skinned and boned leg of pork
(or other lean joint)
4 cloves garlic
1 large onion
1 tbsp brown or raw sugar
Enough beer to cover meat in pot.
(preferably an ale)
1 tspn coarsely ground black pepper
2 tbsp caraway seeds
2 tbsp olive oil
1/2 cup bread crumbs
(preferably freshly made)

Trim any fat the butcher might have left on the pork and prepare the meat for cooking by rubbing it all over with crushed garlic and some black pepper.

Sprinkle the caraway seeds over the meat and press in. They have a fairly distinctive flavour so use just a few if you're at all nervous about them.

In a frying pan, brown the meat all over in some of the oil. Once browned, the meat comes out and the onion goes in. Fry until golden. Add a little more oil if necessary.

Put meat in a heavy pan, top with the onion, and sprinkle on sugar and breadcrumbs, which will help thicken the sauce.

Finally add the beer. For most cooking it's a good idea to use a fairly strongly flavoured beer. Remember the alcohol is evaporated from the beer in cooking so there won't be any left in the final dish. The liquor should now cover the meat. Put the lid on and simmer on a very low heat for about 3 hours.

I find the perfect accompaniment is Witloof, otherwise known as Belgian endive. They are now widely available in

Australia and often used as a salad vegetable.

They can also be cooked although some may find them bitter. The trick to removing the bitterness is simply to cut a slice from the stem end and gouge out the first couple of millimetres, pack snugly in water to which orange juice has been added.

They are delicious and, like most vegetables, low in kilojoules.

When the pork is cooked, remove it to a serving dish and keep it warm.

Add some more breadcrumbs to the sauce if you want to thicken it and pour the sauce over the meat.

Add the witloof and some boiled potatoes and you have the perfect Belgian meal.

EXPLODING A CULINARY MYTH

Browning the meat before roasting or stewing does not seal in the juices, despite what your little old grandmother might have told you. What it does do is give the meat colour and flavour.

JUNIPER PORK

This dish is flavoured with juniper berries from the evergreen tree *Juniperus communis*, which is native to the Northern hemisphere.

It is the very aromatic berry which gives gin its distinctive flavour.

You should have no trouble finding juniper berries in health food shops, better delicatessens and supermarkets.

Serves 4

---

4 lean pork chops, with all fat removed
125 g bacon, with all fat removed

750 g potatoes
1 small glass of white wine or cider
1 onion
2 or 3 cloves of garlic, sliced
12 juniper berries
Parsley for garnish

Peel potatoes and onion and slice thinly. Place half the potatoes and onions in the bottom of an oven proof dish.

Make a small cut near the bone of each chop and insert 2 or 3 juniper berries and slivers of garlic along the cut. Brown chops on each side and place them on top of the potato/onion mixture.

Cover with the remaining potato/onion mixture, sprinkle with the chopped bacon, pour over the wine, place lid on the dish and cook in the oven at 160°C for about 2 hours.

Uncover and garnish with chopped parsley.

A selection of gourmet vegetables make an ideal accompaniment to this dish.

ORANGE GLAZED CHRISTMAS HAM

Christmas is coming, the geese are getting lean.

It's true. Gone are the days when we need to fatten our livestock for Christmas.

When Christmas comes why not celebrate with a magnificent orange-glazed ham.

Most hams are sold already cooked, cured and smoked. But by glazing our ham we can further enhance its flavour, reduce its

fat content and make it look so attractive that you may find it difficult to spoil it by carving.

Serves everyone at Christmas (and then some!)

A cooked ham on the bone
2 or 3 fresh oranges
20 or 30 cloves (yes, really)
1 cup honey
Orange liqueur
(Grand Marnier, Cointreau, or Curacao)

Put the ham skin side up on a rack in a baking pan and remove the rind.

This can easily be done by making an incision around the rind at the pointy end with a sharp knife, leaving just enough rind to use later as a handle.

Using the knife, cut just under the rind at the blunt end of the ham. Then, by putting your fingers under the rind ease it away right back to the pointy end.

The fat can now be pared away with the knife taking care not to cut into the meat itself.

Once that is done cut orange slices about 3 mm thick from the middle of the fruit, reserving the ends to squeeze for juice.

Smear 1 tbsp of honey over the meat. I like to use an Australian wildflower or Tasmanian leatherwood honey.

One by one, place the orange slices over the honeyed ham and fix them in position by gently forcing the cloves through them into the ham, about 5 to each slice.

As well as providing flavour and a delightful appearance, the cloves will stop the slices from slithering down the ham once the honey starts to melt in the oven.

Once covered, the surface can be brushed with the remaining honey mixed with the orange juice squeezed from the reserved orange ends.

Take care not to brush too hard in case you dislodge the orange slices.

Now splash over a little orange liqueur. The alcohol will of course be cooked off.

Sprinkle with raw or brown sugar and place in a moderate oven (about 180°C) for 1 hour.

Baste every 15 minutes with the honey and orange mixture which has dropped into the pan.

When the ham is removed from the oven do a final basting and allow to cool before carving.

An easy way to carve is to hold the pointy end, cut out a wedge, then carve slices downward, finally removing them by cutting across the top of the bone.

Now that you've spoilt your work of culinary art by carving it, serve it with hot or cold vegetables.

VEAL ILLAWARRA

One of the most interesting dishes I have eaten was thirty thousand feet up in an aircraft!

It was the inspiration of Brian Ferguson, Corporate Executive Chef for Australian Airlines.

It features some genuine Australian bush tucker, Illawarra plums, which are becoming increasingly available in the market place.

3 kg loin veal stripped of all fat
1 tbsp canola (rapeseed oil)
Apples (500 g fresh and 100 g dried)
100 g pistachio nuts (shells removed)
100 g red bean paste
Seasoning of pepper and lemon juice
2 or 3 Illawarra plums*
Glass of port
2 or 3 tspn Hoisin sauce

Cut a pocket in the veal (or you can ask the butcher to do it).

Brown the veal in canola oil and remove to dish.

Combine chopped fresh and dried apples, pistachio nuts, red bean paste, Illawarra plums and seasoning. Put in a food processor and mix to a crumbly consistency.

Pipe mixture into the pocket in the veal (or force in with fingers).

Tie joint with butchers' string and roast for 25 minutes per kilogram at 180°C.

To make the sauce, deglaze the pan with port then Hoisin sauce.

Brian serves with a selection of stir fried vegetables.

* Not a problem if not available. The dish will be delicious, it just won't be 'Veal Illawarra'. I suppose it could be called... 'Veal Without Illawarra', in which case use prunes instead.

APRICOT VEAL

This dish also works well with pork.

Serves 4

4 thick veal chops
1/4 tspn ground ginger
Freshly ground black pepper
2 tbsp olive oil
2 small onions, finely chopped
1 tspn tomato paste
1/2 cup red wine
8 canned apricot halves
3 tbsp fine dry breadcrumbs

Preheat oven to 160°C

Season chops with ginger and pepper. Brown over high heat. Place in an ovenproof dish and surround with chopped onions. Discard any fat. Add tomato paste and wine. Pour this mixture over chops. Cover with apricot halves, sprinkle with breadcrumbs. Cook for 45 minutes.

Serve with fresh green beans, steamed baby carrots and lots of rice.

BARBECUED LAMB GREEK STYLE

Yoghurt, lemon and garlic give this dish its magic.

Serves 8

600 ml tub of natural low fat yoghurt

Juice of 2 lemons

1/4 cup olive oil

4 cloves garlic

2 kg lamb (top of leg) with all fat removed and cut into 5 cm cubes

Black pepper

2 or 3 rosemary sprigs

Make a marinade with yoghurt, lemon juice, olive oil, garlic, black pepper, and rosemary. Stir meat chunks into mixture and refrigerate overnight.

Shake off surplus marinade and thread meat onto skewers. Cook on barbecue, basting with leftover marinade each time the meat is turned.

Don't overcook it.

Serve with raw onion rings, a large green salad, basilled tomatoes (see recipe on page 39) and fresh crunchy bread.

HONEY PORK

Sweetened pork for sweeter moments.

Serves 4

500g pork fillets

1 tbsp tomato pureé

2 tbsp honey

Pinch of five spice powder

2 tspn salt-reduced soy sauce

750g broccoli, cut into florets

THE SAUCE

1/2 cup chicken stock

1 tbsp dry sherry

2 tspn honey

1/2 tspn oyster sauce

Pork Kebabs (recipe page 106)

Gestoofd Varkensstuk (recipe page 107)

Orange Glazed Christmas Ham (recipe page 109)

Osso Bucco (recipe page 119)

In a bowl, combine the tomato pureé with half the honey, five spice powder and soy sauce.

Add pork fillets and turn to coat evenly. Cover and refrigerate for at least 1 hour.

Drain pork and place in a baking dish. Reserve marinade.

Bake in moderate 200°C oven for 20 minutes.

Brush fillets with remaining honey on both sides, bake for a further 5 minutes.

Remove from oven and allow to stand 5 minutes in warm place.

Meanwhile, combine the sauce ingredients in a saucepan, stir over medium heat until reduced to thickish sauce.

Cook broccoli by boiling or steaming for 3 minutes. Place in a serving dish.

Cut fillets into thick slices, place on top of broccoli and keep warm.

Pour sauce over pork and broccoli and serve with plain boiled rice.

PORK CHARLIE I

A hint of history in a recipe I've adapted from the sort of fare which was served in Britain during the reign of Charles I.

It features a tantalising mixture of orange, nutmeg, rosemary, and nuts in a stuffing for a lean loin of pork.

It's seasoned with anchovies, which were widely used at the time.

Interestingly, they do not give a fishy flavour to this dish.

Serves 6-8

1 lean loin of pork, about 2kg (ask your butcher to cut it open)

1 tbsp olive oil

1 large onion

50 g pistachio nuts

A few sprigs of rosemary (or 1/2 tspn dried)

1/2 tspn grated nutmeg

Grated peel and juice of 1 large orange

3 anchovy fillets

Breadcrumbs (1 day old)

1 egg

Blend or chop finely the onion, rosemary and pistachio nuts.

Stir in egg, grated nutmeg, orange peel, juice, and anchovy fillets.

Slowly stir in breadcrumbs until the mixture becomes firm.

Put stuffing in the loin and roll up the joint.

Tie with butcher's string or pin closed with skewers or satay sticks.

Smear with oil and roast in oven at 200°C for 1 1/2 hours, basting from time with pan juices.

May be served hot or cold.

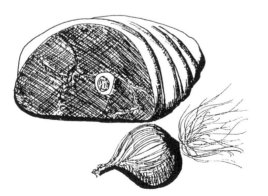

DAUBE MARSEILLAISE

Although daubes, carbonnades and casserole dishes using red meat may have become somewhat unfashionable, this dish can be served with confidence and pride at any winter lunch or dinner party.

It is guaranteed to become a perennial favourite.

Serves 6 to 8

1 kg lean beef cut into large cubes and trimmed of all fat

1/2 litre good red wine

2 cloves crushed garlic

1 sprig thyme

(or 1/2 tspn dry thyme)

2 bay leaves

2 tbsp wine vinegar

2 cloves

1 diced onion

1 tbsp chopped parsley

The day before you want to serve this dish marinate the meat pieces in a mixture of red wine, vinegar, garlic, thyme, cloves, bay leaves, parsley, and diced onion.

Cover and refrigerate.

The next day...

4 rashers of bacon, cut into pieces with all the fat removed

1 tbsp olive oil

1/2 cup brandy (warmed)

2 strips of orange rind

Put oil in a large pan and fry bacon pieces.

Drain meat reserving the marinade before browning over very high heat with bacon.

Pour in pre-warmed brandy and flambé. When the flame has died down, pour in the marinade.

Stir gently and transfer to a casserole dish, add orange rind and cover.

Put in slow oven (150°C) to cook for 3 to 4 hours.

Check it every hour or so to make sure that it doesn't dry out. If it does, add warm water.

It's done when the meat melts in your mouth. Season to taste.

Serve with boiled potatoes and a combination of steamed green vegetables.

LAMBURGER

A real Aussie burger. These are simple to prepare and an alternative to the humdrum beef versions found in the ubiquitous 'take aways'.

Makes 8 burgers

1kg minced lean lamb

1 tspn Tabasco or chilli sauce

2 cloves garlic, crushed

1 egg

150 g cooked rice

1 tspn curry powder

2 tspn cumin

2 tspn Dijon mustard

1/2 tspn pepper

Mix all ingredients together and leave to stand for at least 1/2 hour to allow the flavours to develop in the meat.

On a floured board, roll into burger shapes about 2cm thick. Grill for about 5 minutes on each side.

They taste great served on a slice of home made bread fresh from the oven, with Basilled Tomatoes (See page 39) and a big green salad.

LAMB'S A' CUMIN ✓

This delightful interpretation of the humble lamb roast comes from provincial Morocco.

The Moroccans are fond of lamb and in this dish combine it with one of their favourite herbs, cumin.

Serves 6 hungry shepherds

1 leg of lamb (about 2.25kg) with all the fat trimmed off

15 cloves garlic, peeled (Don't be a garlic wimp!)

2 tbsp olive oil

2 tbsp ground cumin

Prepare the lamb by making deep incisions in it with a thin, sharp knife.

Peel and cut 10 of the garlic cloves into halves. Insert a half into each incision.

Crush the remaining garlic cloves and mix with the olive oil and cumin.

Rub this mixture over the outside of the lamb.

Roast in the oven at 180°C for 1 1/2 hours or until the outside is crusty and brown.

Remove from the oven, place on a serving platter and allow to stand for 10 minutes before carving into thin slices.

Serve with plain boiled, steamed or microwaved potatoes, raw onion rings and salad with yoghurt dressing. (See page 78.)

Tip: A roast joint should be allowed to stand for 10 minutes after removing it from the oven. This allows the meat to settle and will keep it more tender.

EASY SUMMER PORK

This is a new version of an old favourite. We have all had pork served with apple sauce before, now try this for an exciting dish that is easy to prepare.

The pleasure of this dish is that it does not take all evening to prepare.

A good idea for late summer dinners, when tennis takes priority over cooking.

Serves 4

*500 g boneless pork shoulder steaks
with all the fat removed*

1-2 cloves of garlic, crushed

1 dspn of chopped, fresh rosemary

2 tbsp olive oil

100 g button mushrooms, thinly sliced

1 crisp, green apple, thinly sliced

1/2 bunch of spring onions, chopped.

1/2 cup of apple juice or cider

Cracked black pepper

Rub the steaks with the crushed garlic and sprinkle with pepper.

Pat on the rosemary, making certain it is evenly spread. Fry gently in one tablespoon of oil, turning only once, 8-10 minutes on each side.

Transfer to a serving dish and keep warm in the oven.

To make the sauce, add remaining oil to the juices in the pan.

Toss in the sliced mushrooms, apple and spring onions and cook over a medium heat for about 2 minutes.

Spoon the mixture over the steaks.

Pour the apple juice or cider, seasoned with pepper into the pan.

Reduce over a high heat for 2-3 minutes. Pour over the steaks.

The result is a crisp, flavoursome sauce of tasty mushrooms and apples with plenty of life left in them.

Serve the steaks with baby vegetables, perhaps carrots with their tops still on, and boiled, tiny potatoes.

GREEK ROASTED LAMB

A delicious way to jazz up the family roast and certainly good enough to serve at a dinner party.

Serves 6-8

*2 kg leg of lamb, with all the fat
removed*

2-3 garlic cloves

Juice of two lemons

2 strips of lemon rind

1 tbsp fresh or 1 tspn dried oregano

1 tbsp olive oil

1 cup chicken stock

Be sure that the leg is wiped. Cut small incisions in the surface of the leg.

Cut the garlic cloves into slivers and insert into the slits then rub the entire surface with lemon juice.

Sprinkle with oregano and place on top of lemon rind in a roasting pan. Cook in medium oven.

After 1 hour, drain off excess fat and add stock.

Cook for a further hour. Turn during cooking so that it is evenly browned. Drain off any fat.

Allow lamb to stand for 10 minutes before serving with steamed potatoes, pumpkin and sugar snap peas.

SOUVLAKIA

A celebrated Greek dish most of us are familiar with in its take-away form.

Serves 6

1.25 kg lean boned lamb, cut into 2cm cubes

2 tbsp mint, finely chopped

MARINADE

1/2 cup olive oil
1/2 cup dry white wine
Juice and finely grated rind of 1 lemon
3 cloves of garlic, crushed
Finely ground black pepper
1 tbsp fresh or 1 tspn dried oregano
1 onion, grated

Mix marinade ingredients and allow meat to marinate for 12-24 hours, turning occasionally. Drain and thread onto wooden skewers that have first been soaked in water.

Grill or barbecue, turning and brushing with marinade from time to time. Garnish with chopped mint and serve with plain rice and a tomato salad.

OSSO BUCCO

Osso bucco is one of Italy's classic meat dishes. A beautiful blend of veal, vegetables and wine patiently simmered and usually served with the equally renowned Italian rice dish risotto, and garnished with a gremolata.

Ask your butcher for an osso bucco cut. Allow about 1/2 kg per person since much of the weight is in the bone and marrow which add to the flavour.

Serves 4

2 kgs osso bucco (veal or baby beef)
Plain flour for dusting shanks
2 carrots, sliced
1 large onion, finely chopped
1 leek, cut into thin rings
1 tin tomatoes
1 stick celery, finely chopped
3 or 4 cloves garlic, finely chopped
2 tbsp extra virgin olive oil
2 strips lemon rind
1 glass white wine
2 tbsp brandy (optional)
500ml chicken stock
Basil and/or oregano leaves
Black pepper

Using a heavy cooking pot, gently simmer onion, leek, carrot, celery and garlic in half the olive oil until onion has softened.

Dust shanks with flour. Shake to remove excess. Remove vegetables from the pot.

In the remaining oil, quickly brown veal shanks, a few at a time.

If you opt to use the brandy - and I sincerely hope you do as it improves the flavour and is a lot of fun - now is the time to flambé the meat.

Put all shanks in pot and turn up heat.

Warm brandy, strike a match. Pour brandy over shanks and touch flame to the vapours. Be careful of eyebrows and low flying aircraft!

If there wasn't enough heat to flame it, it doesn't matter, the brandy flavours will infuse into the meat and the alcohol evaporate.

Pack the shanks in a casserole dish as tightly as you can to stop them falling apart as they cook.

Put vegetables and lemon rind into

casserole dish.

Add wine, stock and tinned tomatoes which have been broken up.

Add a few basil and/or oregano leaves and a little black pepper.

Cover with tight fitting lid or foil and put in oven at 160°C for 2 1/2 hours.

GREMOLATA

*Combine grated rind of 1 lemon,
2 cloves of finely chopped garlic and 2
tbsp chopped parsley*

Serve with rice, steamed broccoli and a sprinkling of the gremolata.

MOROCCAN BEEF

A tantalising combination of traditional Moroccan spices and 'beefed up' with prunes and roasted almonds.

Serves 6 to 8

*1.25-1.4 kg beef cut in 4cm cubes
2 large Spanish onions, peeled and
coarsely grated.*

1 tbsp olive oil

*1/2 tspn each of freshly ground black
pepper and powdered saffron*

1 tbsp powdered cinnamon

1/4 tspn powdered ginger

450 g dried prunes

4 tbsp sugar

1 strip of lemon peel

2-3 short cinnamon sticks

225 g roasted almonds

Sprigs of fresh mint

Mix the meat cubes in a large bowl along with the onions, olive oil, black pepper and spices.

Mix well, by rubbing the spices into each piece of meat with your fingers.

Transfer the prepared meat to a thick-bottomed flameproof casserole and add just enough water to cover the meat.

Cover and cook over a medium heat until meat is tender, about 45-60 minutes.

While this is cooking, prepare the prune sauce:

Remove a cup of juice from the casserole, place in a small saucepan and remove any fat.

Add half the sugar, the lemon peel and cinnamon sticks.

Cook prunes in this mixture for 20 minutes or until they are soft and swollen.

Transfer meat to serving dish and garnish with prunes and their sauce.

Reduce remaining sauce in casserole to half its original volume over a high heat, then pour over meat and prunes.

Sprinkle with roasted almonds, and garnish with sprigs of fresh mint.

Serve on the spot with brown rice and steamed baby zucchini, squash and carrots.

RABBIT WITH 39 GARLICS

The French have developed several recipes using 40 garlic cloves, presumably the number was chosen on religious rather than culinary grounds.

Since we are not in France, and most Australians are less comfortable about using large quantities of garlic, I have compromised in this recipe, which could equally well be done using poultry.

Serves 4

1.5 kg rabbit, cut into large pieces
39 cloves fresh garlic in skins
1 large onion, finely chopped
500 ml Australian red wine
2 tspn Dijon mustard
1 tbsp olive oil
*1 tbsp each fresh thyme and rosemary
leaves or 1/2 tspn dried*
2 cloves

Wash and dry the rabbit and marinate overnight in wine, cloves and herbs.

The next day...

In heavy pot cook onion in olive oil until

softened. Toss in drained and dried rabbit pieces and brown. Reserve marinade.

Toss in the 39 garlic cloves (with their skins on!) Pour in marinade.

Stir in Dijon mustard.

Cover tightly and cook very, very slowly in oven (140°C) for an hour and a half.

Remove rabbit to serving plate and keep warm.

Remove garlic cloves squeeze them from their skins and smear all over rabbit.

Reduce remaining sauce over high heat and pour over rabbit.

Season with black pepper.

Serve with plain tagliatelle and green salad with very mild dressing.

CHINESE BREAKFAST

Breakfast in China is accorded the same respect as any other meal. This traditional eastern breakfast recipe makes a perfect western lunch.

Serves 4

1 cup short grained rice
2.5 litres chicken stock
300 g pork, rump or topside mince
1 cup spring onions, chopped
1 cup water chestnuts, chopped
(available at most supermarkets)

1 tspn soy sauce.

SIDE DISHES

Bowl of spring onions, finely chopped
Small bowl diced cucumber
Small bowl of sweet Chinese pickle
(available at Asian food stores)

Fresh shredded ginger
Dark soy sauce mixed with a few drops of sesame oil

In a large saucepan bring stock to the boil, add the rice stirring till it comes back to the boil. Reduce heat until it is as low as possible. Leave for 2 hours, the rice will become like a creamy thick porridge.

Meanwhile, mix the mince with spring onions, water chestnuts and soy sauce. Add the meat mixture to rice and beat in. Cook a further 5 minutes. Add soy to taste. Ladle it into bowls and serve with the condiments.

Fruit Desserts

Australians are a fortunate people. Nowhere else in the world is there such a wide range of foods from which to choose and this is especially true in the case of fruit. Previously a nation of predominantly apple, pear and stone fruit eaters, we now have ready access to the fruits from all types of terrain and climate.

Fruits are related to vegetables and many foods that we call vegetables are, botanically speaking, fruits. For example, the eggplant and the tomato. One of the main differences between vegetables and fruit is that carbohydrate exists as starch in vegetables whereas in fruit it exists as sugars.

Apart from the delightful range of tastes and appearances, fruit is a great food because it is a ready source of vitamins and dietary fibre. With the exception of the avocado, they are also low in fat. A further health benefit is the presence in fruit of a little sodium and a lot of potassium.

When buying fruit look for unblemished skin. The fruit should feel heavy for its size. Over-ripe fruit will smell musty.

Fruit is best bought as required and eaten immediately. If it needs further ripening it will do so better in paper bags with a few air holes for ventilation. By putting a ripe banana or apple in with the unripe ones, the ripening process is accelerated.

Try to avoid storing fruits such as apples, pears and stone fruit with their skins touching to prevent bruising.

Always wash fruit in cold water before use, and do not store after being washed since they may deteriorate.

Most fruits will discolour after cutting, a natural process that may be impeded by smearing with any citrus juice. The citric acid will also enhance the fruit's flavour.

The rind of an orange or lemon is also a terrific flavour booster for other foods and enhances many meat and poultry dishes.

Cooking fruit in a sugar solution also prevents discolouring.

Dried fruits may often be substituted for fresh fruits in recipes but it's worth remembering that dried fruit has the same amount of sugar but in concentrated form.

In recipes where butter is traditionally used, canola margarine has been substituted to reduce the amount of saturated fat.

CARAMELISED SUGAR

To caramelise sugar, all you need to do is place equal quantities of sugar and water in a saucepan over high heat and boil until the mixture turns golden, taking care not to burn.

APPLE AND BLUE CHEESE STRUDEL

Ever since Eve tempted Adam with an apple we have been trying to dress up our most popular fruit to make it even more delicious. Of course, most of us have experienced the pleasure of eating apple strudel but how many of us can own up to having a strudel made with blue cheese. It may seem a funny ingredient to put in this traditional dessert, but it makes an enormous difference.

Serves 6

1 kg apples
5 or 6 sheets of filo pastry (the packet variety is perfect)
Light olive oil
1/2 cup brown sugar
1/2 cup fresh breadcrumbs
1 tspn ground cinnamon
50 g blue cheese
Juice and grated rind of 1 lemon
2 tbsp chopped nuts
1 cup sultanas or raisins

Chop the apple into small pieces. I leave the skins on. There is plenty of goodness in the skins and it gives more texture to the strudel. Add the lemon juice. This stops the apple browning and provides nice acidity.

Stir in the lemon rind, brown sugar, cinnamon, breadcrumbs, crumbled cheese, nuts and sultanas. Set aside.

Place damp tea towel on the work bench.

Take five or six sheets of the filo pastry out of the packet and place on the damp towel. Brush the top with a smear of light olive oil.

Next, turn the top sheet over, brush it with some oil. You've now got two sheets which will stick together with the oil but separate to give you the flaky effect during cooking.

Take those two sheets and flip them over to reveal a new sheet which you then brush.

It is now just a matter of repeating until each sheet has been very lightly oiled.

Put the filling on the leading edge of the pastry in a long, neat heap. Fold the side pieces of pastry over the heap.

Roll the parcel up and with the join underneath, place onto an oiled baking tray. Put in the oven at 200°C for about 35 minutes.

Once cooked, allow to cool then dust with a little icing sugar. Serve warm or cold.

ORANGE PANCAKES

The orange was first cultivated in India where it got its name from the Hindi.

They've since become Australia's most popular fruit. Last year we grew around half a billion tonnes, mostly in New South Wales.

Two varieties most commonly found in Australia are the valencia, a summer fruit ideal for juicing, and the navel, a winter fruit that is good to eat.

While we all know the orange is a good source of Vitamin C, what is less known is that only a quarter of this comes from the juice. The rest is in the flesh, the pith and the peel. It makes good sense to use as much of the orange as we can. This recipe does just that!

Serves 4 to 6

THE PANCAKES

250 g plain flour
2 eggs
600 ml skim milk

Sift flour into a bowl. Make a well in the centre of the flour.

Add the eggs and mix well. Slowly add the milk and beat until the mixture resembles thickened cream.

Heat a large non-stick frying pan. Ladle in mixture to thinly cover the bottom of the pan.

Cook till brown then turn and cook on the other side. Roll up and keep warm in a very low oven (100°C).

THE SAUCE

3 or 4 oranges
4 tbsp raw sugar
50 g canola margarine
3 or 4 tbsp orange liqueur (Cointreau, Grand Marnier or Curacao)

Water

To make the caramelised peel, wash and peel one of the oranges.

Cut the peel into thin julienne strips and blanch by putting into boiling water for a couple of minutes and then draining.

Combine 2 tablespoons of sugar and 3 tablespoons of water in a saucepan and boil until the sugar has dissolved. Add the julienne strips and cook until the water has boiled off leaving the julienne transparent.

After about 10 minutes, remove the peel and spread on lightly oiled plate or marble slab. Allow to cool.

Segment the remaining oranges by cutting the peel and pith away with downward strokes of a sharp knife, following the line of the fruit.

Then cut segments out by cutting alongside the membrane of each one.

When all the segments are removed, squeeze out the central core of membranes to remove last of the juice.

Melt margarine in a frying pan and dissolve remaining sugar.

Add the orange segments and cook till most of the liquid has boiled. Add the orange liqueur.

Once the alcohol has evaporated the sauce will be ready to use - pour it over the prepared pancakes. Sprinkle over pieces of caramalised peel and serve with Ricotta Delight (see page 136).

DRIED FRUIT SALAD

This delightful dessert is based on Khoshaf, a dish popular in the Middle East.

Serves as many as the amount you make!

Dried peaches, pears, figs,
raisins, apples, prunes, and apricots
Pine nuts or pecans
Orange juice
Rosewater

Simply cut up the dried fruits and put in a bowl with some pine nuts or pecans. Pour over orange juice and a tspn of rosewater (many large supermarkets now stock it).

Put in a sealed container in the fridge and

leave overnight. (Make sure the container is well sealed as the rose water is very powerful and tends to spread its aroma about when given half a chance.)

By the next day your fruit salad will be beautifully plumped up. It is particularly refreshing served with a low fat yogurt.

HARVEST PEAR CAKE

"A rose by any other name could be a pear."

It's true, the pear is actually a member of the rose family.

Although it is believed to have originated in Asia, one of the world's most popular pears was first produced in Australia at the end of last century.

Charles Packham had the presence of mind to cross a Bartlett pear with an Yvedale St. Germain and created 'Packham's Triumph'.

The pear is a self-contained health food and this recipe of Judyth Blereau's is one of my favourites.

Serves 8

THE CRUMBLE MIX

50 g canola margarine
1/4 cup dark brown sugar
1/4 cup plain flour
1/4 cup oats
1/4 cup pecan or walnuts

Place all ingredients in a food processor and process until just crumbled.

Set aside.

THE CAKE MIX

125 g canola margarine
1/2 cup dark brown sugar
1 tspn pure vanilla essence
2 eggs
1 cup wholemeal self raising flour
1 cup unbleached plain flour
1 tspn cinnamon
1/4 tspn grated or powdered nutmeg
1 cup soy milk
3 cups pears, cubed
(Leave the skins on.)

Cream margarine and sugar. Add eggs and mix until smooth.

Add vanilla and soy milk. Mix well. Add sifted dry ingredients. Fold in pears and half the crumble mix.

Put into greased 20 cm (8") baking dish, top with remaining crumble mix. Bake at 190°C for 1 1/4 hours.

Tip: When using pieces of apple or pear in a recipe, toss with lemon juice to stop the pieces from browning. The lemon also adds tang to the final dish.

FLAMIN' APPLES

This delectable dessert, stolen from the French, is guaranteed to make a lasting impression on dinner guests.

The ingredients are simple, but the results superb.

Serves 4

225 g granulated sugar
4 apples, peeled and cored
4 tablespoons of raspberry or blackcurrant jam
4 tablespoons cognac, warmed
250 ml water

Apple and Blue Cheese Strudel (recipe page 124)

Harvest Pear Cake (recipe page 127)

Put the sugar and water into a big saucepan, boil for 5 minutes without stirring, until the mixture becomes a syrup.

Cook apples for 10 minutes before removing, place the apples on a serving dish and keep cooking the syrup.

Fill the holes in the centre of the apples with the preserves.

Reduce the syrup for another 10 minutes until it has thickened, but not coloured, and pour over the apples.

Just before you are about to serve them, pour over the warmed alcohol and set alight.

PIE I'D (RECOMMEND)

This recipe is adapted from the classic fruit cobbler of America's Deep South.

If you have trouble with pie crusts, this is the pie I'd recommend, hence its name.

Just about any fruit may be used, fresh, frozen or tinned.

Serves 6

3 cups fruit, peeled, cored, seeded, thawed, whatever

1 cup of sugar (less if you're using fruit which was canned in syrup)

1 cup plain white flour

2 tbsp cornflour

50 g canola margarine

2 tspn lemon juice

Grated rind of lemon

2 tspn baking powder

125 ml skim milk

Mix the fruit with sugar and cornflour. Add lemon juice and rind.

Put into 20 cm diameter deep baking dish or tin.

Pre-heat oven to 190C.

Make a soft biscuit mix by combining flour and baking powder, cut the margarine into the mixture then stir in the milk.

It should be fairly firm.

If too sloppy add more flour. If too crumbly add more milk.

Roll out dough on lightly floured work surface.

Don't overwork the pastry or it will become tough!

Lay the pastry on top of fruit mixture.

Poke the edge of the dough into the baking dish. Put a few incisions into the dough to let the steam escape.

Bake for 35 minutes or until lightly browned.

Y'awl can eat it on its lonesome or wid summit. Soul food, awlright!

MOROCCAROONS

No, macaroons are not relatives of that great Scots dish, MacAroni.

These flourless biscuits probably originated in France, where the best ones were made for two centuries by successive generations of Macaroon sisters.

This recipe is for the macaroons which migrated south to Morocco.

Makes 20

150 g icing sugar
1 small egg, beaten
225 g ground almonds
Zest of 1 lemon, grated
1 tspn vanilla essence
1/4 tspn, powdered cinnamon
A little icing sugar for garnish

Preheat oven to 180°C

In a large mixing bowl, combine icing sugar and beaten egg, beat until mixture goes white.

In another bowl combine ground almonds and the rest of the ingredients. Mix into egg mixture.

Now knead the dough-like mixture in a bowl until it becomes pliable. Cover with a cloth and leave for 15 minutes.

Roll the dough into a long, thin sausage-like shape on a lightly floured surface.

Cut into 20 segments. Then roll each segment into a ball and flatten each ball into smaller rounds approximately 1 cm thick.

Place the biscuits on a lightly oiled baking sheet (remember they will spread out whilst cooking). Sprinkle with icing sugar.

Bake in oven for 15 to 20 minutes.

When golden brown, remove and set aside to cool.

Navels gazing

FREYA POVEY'S ORANGE CAKE

This is one of the tangiest cakes I have ever had the pleasure to eat. It is one of the simplest to make and requires neither butter nor flour.

Serves 10 or more

2 large oranges
250 g ground almonds
250 g raw sugar
5 large eggs
1 tspn bicarbonate of soda
2 tspn orange liquor (optional)

Cook whole oranges in water for 2 hours. Drain, and allow to cool. Chop them into large pieces and blend - peel and pith included.

Beat eggs and sugar until creamed. Add other ingredients.

Line a 20 cm cake tin with baking paper. Pour in mixture and bake in 200°C oven for 80-90 minutes.

Check to see if its done by inserting a skewer. If ready it should come out clean.

Allow to cool and serve.

PEAR AND GOLDEN SYRUP BAKE

As well as being low in kilojoules, pears are high in dietary fibre. When buying them, make sure you buy the firmer ones - they will ripen quickly at home.

This dessert is an old, tantalising favourite. Try it and you will see why.

Serves 4

4 small pears
3/4 cup golden syrup
1/4 cup dark rum
1/2 cup orange juice
1/2 cup water
Peel of 1 orange, cut into julienne strips
A little olive oil

Preheat oven to 180°C.

Peel, halve and core pears. Place in a small, lightly oiled baking dish.

Combine the other ingredients in a saucepan. Stir over a low heat until golden syrup has dissolved, then bring to the boil.

Pour this mixture over the pears. Cover tightly with foil, and bake in the oven for 20 minutes.

Remove foil, baste pears with syrup and cook uncovered for another 10 minutes.

Serve while still hot with plain, low fat yoghurt.

APPLE PANCAKES

These are pancakes with a difference - they are made with the apple in the batter.

Serves 4

125 g plain flour
1 egg
1 tbsp brown sugar
Pinch of cinnamon
1/2 cup apple juice
2 tbsp skim milk
1 apple
1 tspn olive oil

Combine flour, egg, sugar, cinnamon, juice and milk thoroughly.

Peel, core, quarter and slice apple thinly.

Add to the pancake mixture.

Heat a frying pan and when hot, brush with a little olive oil. (Don't let it get too hot and smoke.)

Pour or ladle in apple mixture a little at a time.

When the mixture comes away from the edges, turn over and cook the other side.

TOPPING

Mix 2 tbsp honey thoroughly with 1 small carton of plain, low fat yoghurt

When the pancakes are ready, place a dollop of yoghurt and honey mix on each one, fold over and serve immediately.

CHAMPAGNE COULIS

This light and refreshing dessert is absolutely fat free. It makes use of fruit that is readily available in summer.

Serves 4

2 oranges

2 peaches

2 grapefruit

1 punnet of strawberries

3 tbsp granulated sugar

1/2 cup chilled champagne or sparkling white wine

A few mint leaves to garnish

Peel the oranges and grapefruit and cut away segments (see page 77). Peel and stone the peaches. Cut into wedges, the size of the orange segments. Put to one side.

Make the coulis by blending the strawberries, champagne, and sugar in an electric blender until it forms a thick sauce.

Place 1 large tbsp of coulis on each dessert plate. Arrange fruit on top of coulis and garnish with mint leaves. Serve chilled.

FLAMBÉED STRAWBERRIES

An exciting way of serving strawberries, it may also be applied to other soft fruits such as bananas, peaches and apricots.

Serves 6

1/2 kg strawberries

1 tbsp canola margarine

1 tbsp caster sugar

4 tbsp brandy, cognac or orange liqueur

Low fat yoghurt and chopped nuts for serving

Remove stalks from the strawberries, wash and drain.

Melt margarine in a heavy frying pan. Add sugar and mix well. Pour in 2 tbsp of brandy. Cook for a few seconds.

Toss in the strawberries and warm for 1 minute so they are coated with the mixture.

Turn up the heat, pour in the rest of the brandy which has been gently heated. Set alight.

When the flame goes out, put strawberries in individual bowls and pour the sauce over them.

Serve with side dishes of low fat yoghurt and chopped nuts.

REDOLENT SALAD

"Redolent: Having a pleasant smell, fragrant."

A perfect definition for this red fruits salad.

Serves 4 to 6

200 g red plums

2 punnets strawberries

2 punnets raspberries

1 punnet blackberries

600 g water melon, seeds removed

400 red or black grapes, seeded

60 g sugar

2 tbsp water

2 tbsp Kirsch

Place the sugar and water in a small saucepan, bring slowly to the boil. You must dissolve the sugar in the water before the mixture boils.

If you stir the mixture, only do so until it reaches boiling point, otherwise it could become sugary.

Simmer mixture gently for about 5 minutes, or until syrupy.

Cool, then add Kirsch.

This syrup can be made in large quantities and stored in the fridge.

To make the fruit mixture, quarter the plums and hull the strawberries.

Scoop the flesh from the watermelon with a melon baller.

Place all the fruit in a large glass bowl, cover and chill.

An hour before serving, pour over the syrup and, using your hands, toss all together.

Serve either by itself or with a plain low fat yoghurt.

Alternative fruits to use would be red or black cherries (pitted), red or black currants, or any other red fruits in season.

V. good.

APRICOT CLAFOUTI

A clafouti is a cross between a flan and a fruit-filled pancake. It is made in France, often using fresh cherries.

As cherries have a short season in Australia, I use fresh apricots, peaches or any other seasonal fruit.

Serves 6 to 8

450 g ripe, or slightly over-ripe apricots or peaches, washed

1 1/4 cups skim milk

4 tbsp mild-flavoured honey

3 eggs

1 tbsp vanilla extract

1/2 cup sifted plain flour

1 tbsp olive oil

Preheat the oven to 180°C. Oil a 30 cm tart pan, or baking dish.

Pit the apricots, and chop them into cubes, collecting any juices.

Blend the milk, honey, eggs, vanilla and any juice from the apricots. Add the flour and continue to blend for 1 minute until completely smooth.

Pour into the bowl with the apricots, mix well, and turn into the oiled pan.

Bake for 45 minutes or until puffed and browned. If you are having trouble determining how puffed is puffed and how brown is cooked, stick a knife into the centre. It should come out clean.

Remove from the oven and serve hot or warm, but definitely not cold. Don't be surprised if your clafouti falls a bit when it starts to cool.

RICOTTA DELIGHT

Ricotta is a mild flavoured, low fat cheese which is a good substitute for cream.

It is the perfect accompaniment to any dessert or cake and is especially delicious with Schiacciata. (See page 16)

Enough for 1 Schiacciata

1 cup ricotta
1 tbsp mixed chopped nuts
1 tbsp honey

Mix all ingredients together and serve.

MELON SHERBET SOUP

A deceptive name for a delightful dessert. Good for warm summer days, when melons are easily obtainable and not too expensive.

Serves 4 to 6

THE SHERBET

1 or 2 cantaloupe, rockmelon or honeydew melons.

Juice of 1/2 a lemon
1 cup sweet, strong wine. I use muscat.
1 1/2 cups of granulated sugar
1 cup of water

Put a rather large, metal mixing bowl in the freezer.

Mix the sugar with the water and boil so that it dissolves but don't stir otherwise it will go sugary. When the sugar syrup has cooled, stir in the lemon juice.

Peel and seed the melons. Pureé the flesh in a blender, then strain. Add the pureé to the sugar syrup.

Remove the chilled mixing bowl from the

freezer. Pour the mixture into the bowl and put it back in the freezer.

Beat the mixture for a few minutes with an electric mixer once an hour for 3 hours.

Remove the bowl from the freezer half an hour before serving, put it in the fridge instead. Chill 6 dessert plates.

Just before you are about to serve, whisk the sherbet mixture and add the wine little by little. It should be the consistency of whipped cream.

THE MELON

1 small melon, balled
Caramelised sugar (See page 124)
Mint leaves

Spoon the sherbet onto the cold plates, garnish with melon balls which have been dipped into caramel, top with fresh, mint leaves.

MANGO SORBET

Sorbets are a simple and refreshing dessert, easily prepared in an ice-cream maker.

If you don't have one just put the freezing mixture in a strong container in the deep freeze and stir it up every 20 minutes or so until a desired consistency is reached.

Serves 6 adults or 2 children!

500 g fresh mango flesh
Juice and grated rind of 1 large or 2 small lemons

3 tbsp Australian honey (I like red gum or leatherwood honey in this dish)

1 tsp orange liqueur (Cointreau, Grand Marnier or Curacao)

3 or 4 leaves of fresh mint
2 egg whites

Blend all ingredients except the egg whites.

Adjust the amount of honey, depending on sweetness of mango and sourness of lemon.

Whisk egg whites till peaks form.

Fold egg whites into mango mixture.

Put mixture into ice-cream maker and churn until thick. Or put in freezer and stir every 20 minutes.

Serve with fresh mango.

WEIGHTS AND MEASURES

OVEN TEMPERATURES

	°C	°F	Gas Mark
Very Low	120	250	1
Low	150	300	2
Mod. Low	160	325	3
Moderate	180	350	4
Mod. Hot	190	375	5
Hot	200	400	6
Very Hot	230	450	8

DRY INGREDIENTS

Metric	Imperial
15g	1/2oz
30g	1oz
45g	1 1/2oz
60g	2oz
75g	2 1/2oz
100g	3 1/2oz
125g	4oz
155g	5oz
185g	6oz
200g	6 1/2oz
250g	8oz
300g	9 1/2oz
350g	11oz
375g	12oz
400g	12 1/2oz
425g	13 1/2oz
440g	14oz
470g	15oz
500g	1lb (16oz)
750g	1lb 8oz
1kg (1000g)	2lb

CUP & SPOON

1 cup	250ml/8fl oz
1/2 cup	125ml/4fl oz
1/3 cup	80ml
1/4 cup	60ml/2fl oz
1 tbsp	20ml
1 tspn	5ml
1/2 tspn	2.5ml
1/4 tspn	1.25ml

LIQUIDS

Metric	Imperial
30ml	1 fl oz
60ml	2 fl oz
100ml	3 1/2fl oz
125ml	4fl oz(1/2 cup)
155ml	5fl oz
170ml	5 1/2fl oz(2/3 cup)
200ml	6 1/2fl oz
250ml	8fl oz (1 cup)
300ml	9 1/2fl oz
375ml	12fl oz
410ml	13fl oz
470ml	15fl oz
500ml	16fl oz (2 cups)
600ml	1pt (20fl oz)
750ml	1pt5fl oz (3 cups)
1litre	1pt12fl oz (4 cups)

Index

Bon appetit!